Hell No to Hmmm Maybe

—Considering Counseling? Making an informed and thoughtful decision

Hell No to Hmmm Maybe

Considering Counseling?
Making an informed and thoughtful decision

CAROLYN KLASSEN

Hell no to Hmmm Maybe

Considering Counseling? Making an informed and thoughtful decision

By Carolyn Klassen

Published by Carolyn Klassen, Winnipeg, Manitoba

©2019 Carolyn Klassen

Please note that this ebook may contain hyperlinks to external website which cannot be verified for accuracy of these links beyond the date of publication.

Note: This book is for informational purposes only and does not provide professional advice. It is not intended to replace the professional services of a therapist.

ISBN: 978-1-7751751-9-3

Dedication

To the wise souls who showed up for therapy. You who taught me that even when it feels brutal to walk through the counseling door, you could courageously do it anyway. Your insights have taught me so much.

To Mary, who has drunk gallons of coffee with me every Thursday morning over the years. Our little table is a sacred space of deep belonging for me. You have loved me, challenged me, and laughed with me. You inspire me. I am a better version of me because of Thursdays with Mary.

TABLE OF CONTENTS

Section I

1 Who this book is meant for

You may not need to read this whole book. You have some concerns and so you're wondering if you should go to therapy. You're curious to see if this book can address the internal barriers that interfere with making an appointment for therapy. Someone who cares about you wants you to go for counseling and you simply have never thought therapy would be for you.

Look at the table of contents and check out the chapter titles that resonate with you. This is one of those books, where I'm hoping that even reading 4 or 5 pages makes it worthwhile. For some of you, buying this book to study a single chapter might be worth it. It could change your life. If it does, write me to let me know—I'll read it and get back to you. I promise.

Read just what is relevant.

Maybe someone handed you this book to say, "I think you should go for therapy, and I know you will hate the idea so here is a book to prove you are wrong."

That's harsh.

It's difficult for anyone to have someone that cares about you tell you that you need help.

That probably stung a little.

Or a *lot*.

The temptation is to feel offended. You might even feel the hurt of feeling judged—if you can get past the irritation of being ticked off.

If someone handed you this book, and it carries with it an implied or explicit message that you should be in therapy, you will probably hate reading it.

No one enjoys being told what to do. I feel for you.

It will be offensive if someone gave you this book as a strong hint, or maybe even as part of an ultimatum: **Read this or else!** The natural reactions of resentment, anger, frustration, or distrust are real. And they aren't comfortable.

But what if—just, what if—someone gave you this book because they care so much about you, they are willing to annoy you? Because they want you to get help even more than they want to be liked by you.

You know that, deep inside every one of us, there is a profound longing to be liked. It is no different for the person who gave you this book. That person didn't get up this morning asking: "What can I do today to get you furious with me?" I suspect they may have given it a sober second thought as they analyzed the pros and cons of getting this book to give to you. They weighed the risks.

The person who gave you this book knew you might pull away, and yet they gave you this book because they feel that the possible payoff could be worth it.

Receiving and reading this book may be a softening into the fact that they care about you. They care so much about you they went out of their way to find this book, buy this book, and then risked your anger to give it to you.

What if that person who gave you this book has a perspective that you can't possibly have, and because of their different viewpoint, has an ability to recognize something you can't know?

Perhaps this book from a treasured person in your life actually says this, in code: "I love you and I care about you and I want better for you," in paper form? You may not agree with the thinking behind the giving, but maybe you can still feel the love?

If you're willing to consider that this book is in your hands because someone cares enough about you to invest in the relationship, maybe you'll respond to that expression of care by reading even a chapter or two.

❧

Perhaps you picked up this book because you realize while you don't want to go to counseling, there is this little niggling feeling that maybe, just *maybe*, it could help. Maybe you picked it up because you *are* managing—but your world seems more work than it should have to be. Perhaps you'd like to be closer to loved ones but can't work out how to pull it off. Or maybe you're annoying people and you can't figure out how to stop pushing away those you care about. Maybe you're just feeling stuck. What you had planned didn't happen—and now you don't know where to go next.

It is possible the burden of those anxious feelings or the heavy dread of depression has just become too much. It is possible the meds aren't doing what they're supposed to do. Now the doctor has suggested therapy and you don't know if it is right for you.

The panic attacks are too much. The triggers stir up feelings that are too powerful. The leaden feeling is making getting out of bed too hard. The joy is gone, the patience is short, and the anger an all too ready sledgehammer to push people away.

You can't imagine that therapy will do any good, but what's happening right now isn't so effective either.

The barriers inside of you persist in making the task insurmountable. But there is this little piece inside that is aware there could be "more". That inner Yoda knows that talking through something that you might never have whispered aloud would be a release for you. You would have let go of a tremendous burden that you didn't know was so heavy until it was gone.

There is a little part inside you that dares to question the North American message that says, "I can do it all by myself." Because, sometimes, when you are honest with yourself, you admit that doing it on your own hasn't been all that successful.

Do you, somewhere silent deep inside, have a part that just doesn't want to do this all alone anymore?

I'm wondering if you'll consider reading just a chapter or two, the ones that feel like they might be most relevant.

❧

Maybe your partner has said: "We go to couples therapy, or we're done."

Now, that's a kick in the gut, isn't it?

It's difficult to do something that you've seen no value in, especially with a gun to your head. I call the one giving the ultimatum the "*dragger*"—one spouse drags the other to therapy. The spouse, by default, is the "*draggee*".

Being the *draggee* in therapy feels *awful*. It just does.

Trust me, *it's no picnic for the therapist either.*

You are concerned about being blamed, for being labelled as a bad spouse. Well, it wouldn't feel fair, would it? And being blamed and labelled certainly would not help anyone understand who you are underneath all the stuff your spouse complains about. It's likely that your spouse has been suggesting therapy off and on for years, and you've always put it off. "Not now," or "I don't feel like it," or "It's not that bad. Let's just try harder."

But this time, you detect a tone of utter seriousness to the edict: "Therapy or I'm out of here."

So, you've never thought of therapy, but you value your partner and your relationship enough, that you find yourself considering therapy—almost against your better judgment.

And so, this book ended up in your hands.

Perhaps your daughter, or your spouse or your best friend has attended therapy. They rave on and on about who their therapist is, and what their therapist says, and how the last session went, and what novel and exciting feelings they are experiencing. They are excited about the work they are doing in counseling in a way that boggles.

It's confusing, too. So many of us are raised to believe we should be able to solve our own problems and that we shouldn't "air our dirty laundry". Maybe you've picked up this book to understand who goes to therapy and why, because this newfound passion that a loved one has for the work of counseling just puzzles you.

❧❧

Maybe you have a child or a grandchild or a friend who is attending school to be a counselor or a psychotherapist, and you just don't get it. Maybe you're like my dad—a great guy—but he doesn't completely understand what his daughter does. I mean, I know he's proud of me—but he's also perplexed that I have a thriving practice; that people wait for months to have focused hour-long discussions with me. He finds it fascinating that anyone would pay me to have a conversation as a professional, when people are constantly chatting with each other all the time. My dad is an accountant, and his thinking is, "When you can have conversations for free, why would you pay for one?"

Many of us have grown up in a world where we have been taught to believe that people should just "pull themselves up by their bootstraps". This line of thinking implies: "Don't talk to anyone. Just make the changes." This book can shed some light on the whole counseling process—why folks go therapy, what therapy does, and why so many find therapy life changing. Going to therapy isn't avoiding responsibility; it is accepting responsibility.

❧❧

Use the contents of this book as a springboard for discussion with the person who gave this book to you. Choose an idea that you read about here to start a conversation with your *dragger-spouse*.

Consider highlighting some lines in a chapter and bringing it to your first session of counseling so that your therapist can understand what:

- you are seeking
- terrifies you
- your deepest longings are
- concerns freak you out so much that you're not even sure how you will get yourself on the therapist's couch the first time.

Therapists love to do an effective job, and if you can let them know, as you walk in the door, what part of this book got you there, that probably will be helpful. It will give them a *heads up* on topics they should wait on, or go slowly on. It might help them understand what they should not do as you start your sessions.

You get to be you in therapy.

You know the spots that are exquisitely tender, and you know what buttons that shouldn't be pushed lightly or early. This book may give you language and tools to walk into the therapist's office able to speak proactively in ways that will make the whole therapy venture not only do-able, but have great success.

❧❧

I often talk to clients who have come to therapy after years of resisting the internal messages that say, "DON'T GO TO THERAPY!!"

They have wrestled with themselves. They have continued to struggle with disconnected relationships, with depression or anxiety. They acknowledge the sense that says, "There must be a better path forward!"

It's one thing to know that therapy is a favorable idea in general, or for others.

It's a whole other thing to know that, "Getting a therapist is the direction for me to pursue."

❧❧

Your concerns and questions are important. You aren't strange in having doubts about therapy. You aren't alone in resisting the idea of therapy.

I've listened, because, quite simply—and profoundly—my clients are my teachers. I've listened to their stories and apprehensions, and hearing how they have grown, and how their perspectives have changed. This helps me better understand those who have not yet crossed the therapy threshold.

Everyone is different, to be sure. Your reservations to therapy will be unique to yourself.

But I write what I've learned about the hesitations folks have to therapy that they have shared with me over the years. I will also write about how they talk about those doubts after they have been in therapy a while.

The wisdom in these pages comes from decades of carefully listening to clients—some of whom came only after years of hesitation and resistance. I have been writing a blog on our therapy center's website, <ConexusCounselling.ca> for about 10 years. You can read some of these stories and thoughts on the site. As new clients initially come, they sometimes refer to one of these blogs and how that impacted their decision to come to counseling.

2 What this book is not

This book does not deal with external barriers to therapy—the factors in life that make therapy hard to access. To be sure, those external barriers are real and important. These barriers are, however, beyond the scope of this book. Examples of external barriers are:

- Therapy costs money. Some of you have limited resources and have an inability to pay the fees therapists charge. Some areas have free counseling or offer a fee based on your income on a sliding scale. Those resources tend to be in high demand and often have lengthy waiting lists or strict criteria which can exclude many people who want the services. The counseling that you long for is beyond your reach because of cost.

- Therapy costs time. Maybe you are a single parent with two jobs, drowning in your own challenges and those of your children. You might be a graduate student with a job on the side and you're overwhelmed by assignments and to do lists that get longer and longer no matter how many items you try to tick off. Therapy is an investment of time: not only for the time in session and the travel to and from the therapy office, but also the time processing the session.

- People who live in remote locations often don't have access to qualified and competent therapy within their area. You may have some unique circumstances in your life where you feel that local resources are not sufficiently skilled or sensitive. Issues like race, gender, sexual orientation, eating disorders, trauma may need a more specialized approach than your area can offer.

Those external barriers need addressing.

Absolutely.

I trust that you will be creative in knocking on doors, developing alternatives, and advocating for the help you need to create the space required to do the work.

Don't give up on your own healing.

Please.

Your suffering matters. Your story needs witnessing.

You are too important not do to what it takes to be the best person you can be. The contribution you make to this planet is vital. You are uniquely gifted. You have a unique place amongst your family and friends that allows you to influence them in ways that only you can do.

∾∾

This book doesn't help you decide who you should see.

If you think you might need medications, and you haven't had a physical checkup in some time to rule out biological factors that impact on your mental/emotional/psychological health, start with talking to your family doctor.

Social workers, psychologists, psychiatrists, psychotherapists and marriage and family therapists can provide counseling. Some spiritual leaders like priests, pastors, rabbis or imams may be helpful for counsel. It's often helpful to check around on the internet to determine who might be best for you. There is absolutely no way to replace positive recommendations from people you trust.

Word of mouth is a fantastic way of finding a therapist good for you. Maybe the best way.

Research to find the appropriate therapist/counselor. Find out what model of therapy the clinician uses and determine if that works with your needs. Do what you can to determine a good "fit" between yourself and the clinician. Carefully explore the years of education, the amount of experience they have in dealing with your focus, and to which professional associations they belong. Make sure they have a solid reputation.

Don't settle.

More than anything, though, ensure that you feel that the therapist/counselor can help you. Does s/he inspire confidence? Do you feel respected? Does s/he listen well to you? Are your concerns heard thoughtfully? Do you feel you can work with him/her? Can s/he disagree with you and challenge you in a way that has you feeling like it is in your best interest? That the hard moments in session are worthwhile moments? If you bring up a problem with the therapy itself, does it get addressed and then resolved in a way that increases your trust in him/her? Do you leave with a fresh perspective?

The most critical factor in choosing a great therapist is feeling s/he is a good fit for what you need.

This book doesn't help you pick out who you should see, although by reading its pages, you may discover a developing awareness of qualities and skills you want your therapist to have. There are plenty of ways to explore and determine who could be right for you. Talk to friends, go online— attempt finding the right therapist rather like you might pursue finding and purchasing the right car.

Simply put, allow the process to take some time, some consultation and some research.

It's not realistic to expect that everyone will find the ideal therapist who is just perfect for them the first time. Sometimes, you do a *test drive*, and you find it simply isn't going to work. It is every client's hope that the therapist they start with will be one that will allow them to do the work effectively. But it doesn't always happen.

I suspect that the only thing harder than starting therapy for the first time is initiating therapy a second time after a bad encounter.

It's hard when you feel you don't "click" with a therapist immediately. It's a great experience when you feel the "click" even in the first session. That happens, but not always. Rest assured, finding that it will not work with a particular therapist is as normal as trying on a pair of shoes at the store and not having the first ones you try on be comfortable. Sometimes a second session with a therapist is helpful when you had a bad first impression to effectively determine if this is someone you can work with.

If you feel talked down to, or judged, or feel you are being told what to do in ways that stop the process—and when you raise this concern, the therapist doesn't candidly discuss the matter in ways that resolve it well for you, give yourself permission to try again.

Your personal growth is too important to allow a bad encounter to turn you off from therapy. Pursue therapy again, knowing that you have learned something from a session that didn't feel right. When you see another therapist, it might be helpful to let the new therapist know that you had an adverse experience, or that, somehow, therapy didn't *fit* with that other therapist.

❦

This book is **not** about coercing you into therapy. It's not about guilt tripping you to do something that isn't right for you. (Though someone may have given you this book hoping it will have that effect on you!) This book seeks to create a respectful space where I can give you some different ways of thinking about therapy.

I invite you to read these pages with curiosity. Curiosity is an openness to learn and explore. It means setting aside judgment (which implies a decision has already been made), which can be hard for all of us to do.

So, I don't want you to think I'm telling you to go to therapy. I don't know you and I cannot possibly know what is right for you. But I have been doing counseling for about 20 years and have been speaking to reluctant therapy attenders for that long too. Just as plumbers know more than I about plumbing, and mechanics know more about cars than the average person, I know more about counseling than most. I'm inviting you to listen in on some things I've heard and thought about.

Can you do me the favor of not deciding before you read this book that you know counseling is wrong for you? Suspend your decision and explore only the chapters in this book that feel relevant to where you are right now.

Be curious about what happens as you read through these pages:

- Is there one story that brings tears to your eyes?
- Is there a page that makes you especially angry?
- Is there a chapter you know you *must* skip because you don't want to know what it says?

Notice these reactions inside of you and wonder what is underneath them. Be gentle with yourself as you explore what is happening. Slow your reading down and just be with your thoughts and feelings. You might think *the noticing* sounds hokey—ok, I'll give you that. But wouldn't you want to know what's happening? Isn't that better than ignoring something important that might just be happening? What if your response to what you are reading is an important key that may unlock something inside of you? Don't we all long to be free of that which holds us back?

This book is not therapy.

It explores why people go to therapy and intends to set you off in the right direction, but it isn't *intended to replace* going to therapy. This book addresses concerns that myself and my colleagues frequently hear. Some of these are put-up fronts to avoid therapy, some of them are legitimate considerations that need addressing in therapy. Others are simply excuses that need to be named as excuses to allow you to go underneath to discover why they thrown out as reasons not to attend.

Please don't confuse this book as therapy in itself. It's merely an arrow that points towards therapy in a helpful direction.

A few notes:

Counseling and therapy are used interchangeably throughout this book. In some circles, counseling can denote discussions that involve more casualness. Sometimes, counseling can connote advice giving. People often perceive "therapy" as more professional and clinical. However, both terms are about spending time with someone who recognizes you as the expert of your story and comes alongside as the expert of the process. As you read, please extend grace if you have a preference for either the term "therapy" or "counseling" over one of these other terms. You're welcome to mentally substitute one term for another.

In the United States, "counseling" is spelled with one "L" and in Canada, "counselling" has 2 "L's"—for consistency, one "L" will be used.

Most of the stories I tell are about me or about friends and family who have given me permission to tell these stories. I have used very few general and generic illustrations of clients. Please know that I have amalgamated stories and changed all identifiers so they are no longer about any individual client. The details change information to completely preserve confidentiality but allow me to continue to make an important point.

Regardless of how this book ended up in your hands, know that I am honored to walk a short bit of your life with you as you contemplate a few of these pages. Know that I understand that it took you courage to accept this book or seek this book, and that I picture you right now reading it as I write these words.

As I picture you reading these words, I smile a little. I like to visualize that a brave person has chosen to consider doing something challenging. I respect folks deeply who value their own growth, and value the impact that they have on others, and are willing to invest in uncomfortable conversations and activities to do just that.

Also, know that I understand that you might feel like a hot mess right now as you read, and the words on these pages don't help. It might feel like the stories and thoughts only serve to turn up the heat in your life, when it already feels like you're getting cooked.

I've been accused, occasionally, of mind reading.

For the record, I can't.

However, it might feel like I'm *all up in your business* at times. I've had the profound privilege of listening to people speak vulnerably and deeply to me. They tell me things that I've thought myself. They echo the words others have said to me, even though they have never dared speak them out loud before. So often, many are so ashamed of deep thoughts that they have never shared out loud—and then are surprised when they see them on a page, not knowing that anyone else thinks these profound, private thoughts too. We all have far more in common with each other than most people would ever know.

I hope you can find your heart in one of these pages, recognize it, and allow yourself to feel understood.

Read what you can, when you can, and give yourself permission to put it down to take a deep breath, go get a glass of water, or walk around the block.

Know that you may need to put this book on the shelf for a few months and then take it off to read again in a while.

The invitation these pages extend to a fuller life is maybe just a little too much, considering all that is going on right now. Know that you will be able to pick it up again, when the time is right.

Be aware, as corny as it sounds in a book, I am delighted that you would read these words to make an important, potentially life changing choice.

And, most of all, know that I wish you well, regardless of what decision you make about therapy.

Section II Real reasons **not** to go for counseling

As a therapist, you may think I am biased towards the helpfulness of therapy.

That's a fair assumption.

I have conversations daily that folks use towards changing the direction of their lives to be more compassionate towards themselves. They seek to connect better with their spouses or children and engage more fully and vitally with their jobs/hobbies/interests. I love spending my days watching brave people make choices to do things differently, allowing for change and growth.

But I also don't think therapy is right for every situation.

As a matter of fact, I believe there are circumstances where therapy is not the best choice. At times, (though not as often some people would prefer), therapy can be a poor choice, and even, sometimes, do harm.

A couple of years ago, an acquaintance of mine got dumped by her husband. They got married less than a year prior. This couple had dreamed and planned for months before the ceremony, planning a future and a life together. They bought a larger home that they intended to renovate to create their nest together. It had a mortgage to match the increased square footage.

He walked away from the house, his wife and his life, just after they moved in.

She, frankly, was devastated. Her kids were confused, and she was crestfallen that the man she thought would be a permanent figure in their lives had bailed on her children too.

She had good friends who were deeply concerned about her, understandably. They asked me to hang out with her on a Sunday morning for an hour because they were concerned she would choose to end her life. They were scared for her. Her friends had good reason to be concerned. She was in a bad way.

These friends of hers were also generous—and they talked amongst each other and collected money. They gave it to her so she could see a therapist for several sessions.

She took the money and bought paint.

She painted her bedroom in this house that was brand new to her—the master bedroom that they had imagined would be their room together when they bought the place. The bedroom that she would now sleep in alone. It got painted a girly colour that she loved and he never would have chosen. She went thrift shopping and discovered some awesome pieces of furniture to put in the room and quirky art for the walls. She spent the weekend creating a cozy nest for just herself that she knew she would love being in.

She explained to her friends that painting the room was therapy for her. She's an artsy type and putting fresh paint on the wall signified hope when life felt bleak. Changing the color was saying she was going to actively embrace the new opportunities life now offered—even though it wouldn't be anything she would have chosen.

She told them that the best way to spend the money was to create a space that felt peaceful and safe and cozy—a place that celebrated her unique identity. It was a space where she knew she belonged.

Who were we to tell her she was wrong?

Sometimes, doing the life-giving thing is, in fact:

- going on a long trip away
- engaging in comforting and creative pastimes such as woodwork, painting, journaling or pottery
- taking an extended break from life, or

- simply embracing the mundane routine that gives rhythm and meaning to life.

Therapy isn't always necessary. There are certainly times when you realize what the best thing is for you to do to get through a rough patch. If you know what you need for healing—do it!

Therapy is about being in a space where there is deep and meaningful connection with another human being. The encounter is life altering. However, you may already have the life-giving connections that you need to get through this time. If you are honest with yourself about the quality of those connections—because you can be candid and receive help from those around you—therapy may be unnecessary.

3. You have a supportive community around you

Therapy didn't exist even 200 years ago—except perhaps for the very elite. The whole profession has developed rapidly in the last century. This is largely in response to the decreased support that people receive in their lives.

In the 1950's the size of the typical new home was 950 square feet, up from 750 square feet just after World War II. By 2000, the average new house size is 2,320 square feet![i] North Americans appreciate their space. But all that space to move around in and enjoy—extra bedrooms and bathrooms, extra living areas—all that space also means, very practically, that there is more distance between people.

People move away from family to get a job. They move between cities ripping up roots to start new one. They live in suburbs distant from those with whom they grew up. In this world of hyper-connectivity with cell phones in everyone's pocket, people might appear more wired into each other. In fact, most spend more time watching YouTube and Netflix than in meaningful conversations around board games or going for long walks with a friend.

Everybody needs connection—especially when working through difficulty. And we all have difficulty. While therapists provide valued and skilled connection in difficult circumstances, sometimes, the listening ear is best in community. Not everybody needs a therapist. Sometimes, a kind friend is even better.

Some circumstances seem big and scary—what they need is the kindness and caring of someone already in their lives.

Maybe you need not get all fancy and book an appointment with a therapist. Maybe what you do need is to get deliberate about creating meaningful connection with the folks already in your life.

❧❧

My youngest son is Jay. His mother died several years ago. The very month he started kindergarten was the month she discovered the breast lump. She had major surgery while he was in kindergarten. Chemotherapy and radiation followed. She was in remission on powerful drugs that affected her everyday while he was in first through third grade. When he was in fourth grade, the cancer came back, this time in her bones. Once it was in the bones, even though she fought hard, it was a losing battle. In the spring, when Jay was in 5th grade, she died.

Car (pronounced "Care") was a wonderful woman. I knew her because our kids played on sports teams in the community over the years. Sometimes on the same team, more often on opposing teams. We used to occasionally catch up on life visiting in the hallways of the gym. Car was fully engaged with life until her death.

Car loved her kids. Planning fancy birthday parties with elaborate home-made cakes and treasure hunts was her thing. She cuddled and played and nourished and nurtured them. Car cared deeply about their friends and their friends' parents. When she died, it was a huge loss for her children—and the community. A loss with so many layers.

The biggest reason she fought against her death was her desire to continue parenting these kids. She loved being their mom, and she didn't want to *leave the party early*.

When she died, there was a huge hole in the household. They all missed her terribly.

Perhaps the hardest part of coping with her death was that she would have been the one to help them through the pain. Car knew what to say and how to say it. She knew when they needed to talk. Car knew how hard to push them to get some of the pain and the hurt now, and wait for more later. Their mother knew how to tend to their hearts. And now when their hearts were broken for her, she wasn't there to help hold the pieces. She knew when to cut them slack for bad behavior because of the loss. And the times when it would have made sense to insist they continue with regular routines of chores she would have said so. Sometimes, sad kids do better following the normal patterns of life.

I'm married to their dad now. I am, what we call in our household, a *bonus parent*. His children and I enjoy each other's company. They like to eat, and I like to cook and bake. That's a good fit! I help with carpooling, and update things on the calendar so everybody gets to where they should go.

But I am *so not* their mother. Because I'm married to their dad, Jim, there is a danger that I could now be seen as their mother. That's *not OK*. Because I'm not. They have a mom, and she's not here. So, I think sometimes, they have to stay extra far away from having tender conversations with me.

Not to mention—what kind of adolescent boy would like that the new bonus parent in the house is a therapist? One more solid reason that I am not a person in which to confide!

Jay is a boy in North American culture. Tell me, how is it that a boy entering adolescence is supposed to grieve? Those middle school years are a time when the school yard eats vulnerability for lunch. It's widely believed (wrongly, by the way) at that age that crying is for wimps. Sharing your heart is something that normal guys aren't supposed to do. And feeling sad feelings in a raw, honest way just isn't seen in popular media. Video games are excellent at numbing out life—but leave little room for feelings one's feelings. We don't give adolescent boys a lot of space to grieve in our culture. The news in our lives moves from one top story to another in a few hours—maybe a day or two. Grieving a parent takes years—which is inconvenient in an instant society. The hole in his life because of his mother's death was huge—and remained unprocessed and un-cried-for.

My husband's and my attempts to create opportunity to have him grieve were well intentioned, but relatively unsuccessful. Jim would take him to the gravesite, or I would make a recipe from her recipe box for supper. Not much response. We wanted to respect his timing and his discomfort with the whole process. I don't think you can push grieving onto anyone. We were aware the grief was there. We could see grief's effects. It leaked through to us via his sullen quietness, the lethargy of hours spent on the couch, his cynicism and sarcasm, and his lack of initiative and engagement.

One evening, we watched a video online of a family friend. Her school had a speech competition and her topic was about her mother's illness and death. The young teen spoke openly and bravely about how this difficult experience changed her. As we noted her own understanding of her grief, it sparked a conversation. Jay was just beginning to be aware of the "dark hole" inside that he was having trouble articulating.

I asked him: "Jay, if I were to make you talk to someone, would you be furious at me and hate me for it, or would you pretend to hate it, but secretly be relieved?"

He told me, "Yes".

Typical teenager—answering multiple choice with a *yes* response! I took it as permission and pressed further.

"Would you rather talk to a counselor or to a mom of one of your friends?"

He told us he preferred a mother and named one of his friend's moms who has often driven him in carpool to practices.

I contacted the mom, Bonnie, the next evening to find out if she would be willing and interested. She said that Jay had already asked her during school pick up that day if I had been in contact with her!

Jaw drop number one!

She willingly agreed to spend time with Jay, her son's friend.

Bonnie arranged a time for her to pick him up the next day. He came home after about 90 minutes—and announced to me: "Carolyn, let me tell you how a grown up gets a 14-year-old boy to talk. You pick up drinks at Starbucks and then just drive around. You don't look at me. You make the drive interesting so we can just look if there's a long time when it's quiet. I need to look at stuff through the window and be a little distracted before I can talk." He added, knowingly: "Just sitting across the table from a boy is not a good idea if you want him to talk."

Jaw drop number two!

He was giving me lessons on how to talk to him.

Lesson noted and learned.

I thanked Bonnie the next time I saw her. Bonnie owns a business with multiple staff. She travels across North America for work. And she took time to meet with my Jay. It moved me. So humbling to have someone be willing to spend time with one of my family for no other purpose that that he wanted to, and he requested her.

Her eyes filled with tears and she gave me a hug. She told me she was so very, very grateful to the many men who had spent countless hours with her son in the gym coaching him. She knows that coaching young boys isn't just about teaching them better ball handling or more strategy to play the game. Bonnie understands that coaching boys is about perseverance, collaboration, and characters. She knows that men coach to help fine young boys become better young men.

Bonnie told me that men had poured into her son's life and she told me how grateful she felt. It seemed as if there was nothing she could contribute to the community and to the children. My husband, Jim, was her son's basketball coach for a few years. She told me she loved the opportunity to meet with Jay because it was a cool opportunity to "pay it forward". Even better, she said she liked Jay and investing in him was a privilege.

She texted me the three conditions she had given Jay when they first started meeting:

1. She wouldn't tell anyone but her husband they were meeting. Jay could tell who he wanted.
2. She would keep the conversations between them private, unless something came up that for safety reasons, his parents would need to know.
3. We should all understand she didn't know what she is doing. She runs a welding company, not a therapy company.

I let her know that we trusted her to listen to him. We trusted her to provide a space where he could begin to wrap language around the very painful experience of losing his mom. We valued her willingness just to be someone he trusted to spend time with the tender feelings he was just beginning to acknowledge.

The next week, I tucked a gift card to a coffee shop on Jay's pillow. I wrote a note inside letting him know that I supported his car rides with Bonnie. He was to let me know when the coffee card needed reloading, and I would take care of it.

I checked in with Bonnie a few weeks later. She told me of a cute moment when an hour into a visit she heard him say something about the upcoming supper. Bonnie took that as "adolescent speak" for "I want to go home for dinner now". She turned the corner towards home, and he said, "Are you taking me home? I thought we had an hour and a half?"

Jaw drop number three.

He was asking to keep talking.

Tears in my eyes.

I know nothing about their conversations—except that their time together is worthwhile. I'm not sure how to put it—but I think Jay as a little *looser.* He's a little more relaxed. Jay is a little more active in conversations. He pushes back a little more sometimes when we ask him about his behavior. Jay is more engaged in his life.

Jay wasn't best served by being with a therapist.

He felt better able to open up with a trusted friend who would be a therapeutic presence in his life. He knew that he had someone already in his circle with whom he felt he could explore the hardest, most painful loss of his life.

Many of us have the gift of someone that can provide a safe space to talk about the hard stuff that is super hard to talk about. May you have someone that you already know that you can trust to listen to you non-judgementally, so you have the opportunity to hear yourself out loud.

If you have even one or two friends in your life that will be curious with you about the painful decision you face, or the complex web of emotions you have, you may well have all you need.

∼∽

So many of our hurts and wounds arise out of the painful relationships we have had. It makes sense then, that healing would come from the caring relationships in our lives. If you are fortunate enough to know someone who has been, or can become a healing presence in your life, professional therapy may well be unnecessary.

Therapists work in your life in an ordinary, human way—through listening, reflecting, empathy, conversation, challenge, providing different perspectives.

Make no mistake—therapists have gone to school for years to become expert at these skills. They have tools in their helping toolbox that others don't have. Just like plumbers and electricians and bakers have tools specific to their trade.

Maybe you don't need the fancy tools—maybe you just need the regular tools that a caring, warm person who wants to listen can provide.

Perhaps someone just listening to you, as you dare to try telling your story is enough. Maybe bouncing your troubling situation off a person who's not a professional but their caring is qualification enough is what you need?

∼∽

Merely having someone in your life that you can lean on and share a challenging situation with isn't enough. Just knowing they are there and would have a conversation with you is one thing—but actually having the conversation with that person is another.

So often, the words get unsaid, the stories are unshared. You may be dying inside, wanting to tell your story. The other person may be kind and compassionate and very willing to listen. But unless the conversation happens, you don't get the benefit of it.

That sounds rather obvious doesn't it?

Often people have the idea that it could be right to talk to someone, but it remains just that— an idea. It requires another whole level of courage to deliberately create the space for these conversations to actually occur.

The person you know would be good to talk to can't read your mind. She doesn't know why you've been preoccupied and quiet, or irritable and testy. He doesn't know that there is a situation going on in your life that preoccupies you.

Or maybe she has an inkling that something is going on for you. But she can't read your mind to know that you want to talk.

You can't read his mind. You can't know what she is thinking. You can't know if the other person has what it takes in time, and internal resources to give you the support you need.

Asking for someone to listen to you is hard. Asking for help is brutal for most of us.

Can you ask for what you need? Can you fire off a text or an email—or even pick up the phone and say, "There's something I need to talk about. I think you might be a good person to listen to me. Do you have time to meet with me? I'm not good at talking, but maybe I could try to talk with you?"

Can you know that if that person says, "Sorry, it doesn't work for me", it's that they have reasons unrelated to your worth as a human being? It's legitimate when people say, "My kids are taking everything from me right now," or "My work has some brutal deadlines," or "I might not look it, but I'm in my own hell of depression right now." There are valid reasons that a person is maxed out and therefore, not able to invest deeply into walking with you during a hard time. It may be too hard for them to give you the reason out loud. I know that you will be tempted to think it reflects poorly on you if you get turned down. It will be hard for you to hear—and then even harder to ask someone else.

However, when you ask someone to be a part of your life in a healing way, you are also implicitly saying, "I trust you and value you. I believe that you have what it takes to help me." That sort of compliment is a gift to the person you will ask. You honor the person you invite into a tender part of your heart.

So, it may be hard to let someone in, but, if you have someone in your life that may be a candidate, can you give it a shot? Can you dare to ask them for help?

- Then keep asking for what you need when you meet with them.
- If it's too hard to look at her when you talk, ask to go for a car ride.
- If you need to keep moving, tell him that you want to meet at the park and walk.
- If you like to hold something with your hands when you talk, meet at a coffee shop and hold a mug.
- If it is best that person just listens, tell her that.
- If he starts saying things that aren't helpful, it's ok to say, "Dude—let me tell my story. Don't give me advice."
- If you don't want them to hug you, let them know.
- If you feel like a hug would be just the thing, don't wait and hope for it—make it happen.

It's OK to teach people what you need.

It might not occur to someone you trust that they need to allow you to tell your story in a way that is meaningful to you, in a style that fits you. Most people relate to others in a style that they think works, because it is what works for them. It's natural for a person to hug you if they think they would want a hug in the same situation. If they are a person who likes to tell a story uninterrupted, they may stay silent out of respect. Unless you know that, you may wonder if they are uninterested or if they are even listening. Give yourselves both a gift by figuring out how to make it work.

Maybe you are like my son, Jay—someone who is having some trouble working through a difficult circumstance. He's doing well in school and has friends. He's actually bumping along through life fairly well—he just misses his mom literally unspeakably much. Jay is fortunate to have a person in his life whom he trusts to confide in—and a bonus parent who was willing to set it up for him. Bonnie made the conversations safe for him. Rather than do the work with a therapist, he's doing it with a friend while driving endless laps around our city park with a grande Iced Tango Passion Tea Lemonade in his hand.

It's working for him.

And *if* it *works* for you too, you don't need a therapist.

4 You are grieving normally (and painfully)

My first pregnancy ended in tragedy.

We were looking forward to being first-time parents. We just finished grad school in California and moved back to Canada for my husband to begin a new position. Eager to become parents, we had forced ourselves to hold off trying to conceive a child so I wouldn't be over 5 months pregnant before we moved to Canada. Our insurance didn't cover the last trimester of pregnancy in the United States.

I was one of those little girls that loved baby dolls and always dreamed of becoming a mother. I was more than ready to become a mom. I was so excited to be pregnant. Friends at the seminary and friends at work both held baby showers for us before we left our California home. I had the stroller waiting for a bundle to push around the block, a baby carrier waiting for an infant to snuggle, little outfits and a teddy bear I couldn't wait to put in the corner of the bassinet. I couldn't wait to be a mom.

We weren't back in Canada long before we became aware one evening that something was very wrong. My obstetrician admitted me to hospital. When she did tests to determine what was going wrong, there was an unexpected turn of events. We discovered that my belly was holding two babies. Twins! But we also discovered that my body was not hosting them well, and they were in terrible danger.

We were delighted, except, now we knew not one, but two, lives were held in the balance. I was on complete bedrest with my head lower than my feet in the bed. For two weeks I lay somewhat upside down, hoping we would have enough time to give these little two the chance they needed to live.

My favorite times of the day were in the morning and evening when the nurse would come and find their heartbeats and we would listen. One little guy's heart rate was steady and constant—the other little guy's heart beat would fluctuate a bunch. That explained the wild rolling on the top left side of my belly! I loved to feel these little guys inside.

The odds were against us, and we knew it. But we hoped that if I did everything right (which meant I would do exactly nothing except incubate these babies) that maybe they would live. We were just starting to believe that these tiny guys might have a chance.

Then, one morning they couldn't find the heartbeats. We all hoped the babies had just moved around and weren't in position for the nurse to detect the rhythmic thumping. They sent me for an ultrasound—and there it was: no heartbeats.

My babies had died in the night.

Nurses and doctors floated in and out of the room as they made arrangements. The resident who was clearly new on the unit, and it seemed, very new to telling expectant mothers that her babies were dead, was awkward—to the max. He shifted his weight from one foot to the other, stood on the very far side of the room very near the door, eager to make his getaway as soon as he blurted out the news. It seemed he met every question we asked with leaving the room to get an answer. He seemed relieved to find reasons to dash out of the room.

The one redeeming bit about this baby doctor, bless his heart, was that his fly was open. He provided some very necessary comic relief. We were devastated and crying for most of the hours following his news. But every time he left the room, my husband and I would notice the current status of his fly (yep, still down!) and lose ourselves in giggles. Sometimes, tears and laughter are very near each other, aren't they?

My body figured out the work it needed to do, and contractions began that afternoon. I delivered two tiny but very perfect babies that evening.

We held Branden Calvin and Matthew Peter and cuddled them for a long time. I still remember trying to memorize their weight, their softness, and of what their fingers and toes were like to look at. I was hazy from all the drugs, but I was determined to imprint that time forever.

The next day, as I left the hospital, they gave me the blankets they had wrapped my sons in when I was holding them.

We invited family and a few friends to gather in our living room later that day with a pastor who said some things, and everybody went around the room and said more somethings. Emphasis on something—likely very kind and thoughtful. However, I have no idea about very much of anything that day. It's all a blur.

Well, that's not exactly true. I remember I sent my husband out to buy blue napkins for the snacks we would eat after the service. I was irrationally passionate that the napkins be light baby blue—no other napkins could possibly work. I believe he needed to go to a few stores to find them. He knew that I would be a crazy woman if he didn't show up with light baby blue napkins. Grief can be funny like that—emphasizing some tiny matter and ignoring other, much bigger things.

The next day was Father's Day. Gosh, it was a punch to the gut to wake up as newly childless. Everyone was celebrating all things fatherhood, and we were mourning two little boys.

The following days, weeks and months were confusing, frightening and exhausting. I didn't know this new me that was now grieving. That was discombobulating—to feel like a stranger to myself. I've always been a fairly optimistic, cup-half-full sort of person. Now, I was grumpy and hopeless. Nothing seemed fun.

Color had drained from my world and I lived in shades of grey.

I didn't know what to do with myself.

Television shows and movies just seemed silly. What was the point?

I tried to read. Reading was always a favorite pastime. But now I could read the same paragraph over and over and it just wouldn't make sense. I remember taking a Little House on the Prairie book out of the library, hoping that its basic reading level would help it be comprehensible to my brain.

Friends would come over but I wouldn't know what to say. It was hard to watch people coming and going, enjoying all that goes on in the daily grind of life. Didn't they know my world had fundamentally changed? How could they go on as if everything was normal? I was angry and sad and confused—and then upset with myself that I made little sense.

In the mornings, I would often have 2 or 3 seconds before I remembered that I lived in a world where my children weren't alive. I would feel blissfully normal for a few fleeting seconds. That was immediately before the oppressive cloud of grief would weigh on me again. And then I would be angry at myself that even a few seconds had passed where I hadn't grieved. And I would feel guilty that those few seconds had been wonderful—and angry at myself that I wanted more of them.

I fell asleep crying for a lot of nights. It was miserable.

I remember thinking there was a distinct possibility that I was going crazy. As in, *not sane.* That's not written lightly as a sarcastic, disrespectful line which denigrates those with mental illness.

I remember being genuinely concerned I was entering a mental state from which I would never recover.

I went to a workshop a decade ago on depression. The psychologist leading the workshop was talking about signs and symptoms, treatment, and all matter of things related to depression.

He described going to New York, as so very many helping professionals did, in the aftermath of 9/11. The buildings had fallen, and thousands were reeling in the devastation of the terror of that day. He spoke of going to a New York fire house, and being surrounded by the remaining surviving firefighters, some of whom watched the towers fall on their comrades. The families of those who were killed trying to save the lives of others were also there. He described the incredible pain of those in the room. Firefighters had lost multiple colleagues, some of whom they had spent years working with. Family members lost dads, brothers, husbands.

The bottom had dropped out of their world.

The room oozed with a terrified vast ocean of grief that everyone was swimming—or rather, drowning in.

This psychologist related the essence of what he delivered to those in the room in the firehouse that day:

I'm here because I care and I want to support you in your grief. All of you have lost someone important to you. Some of you have lost many important to you. Grief is agonizingly painful to feel. It will create periods of confusion, anger, uncertainty, feeling lost, loneliness and so on. However, I am not here because there is anything wrong with these feelings. I am not here because what you are feeling is a problem. You are having very normal and very understandable reactions to huge loss. I am here because I want to help. I am not here because there is anything wrong with what you are feeling. While the tragedy of 9/11 is utterly wrong, feeling the grief you have is not wrong. Go ahead and be heartbreakingly sad. Allow yourselves to feel the full range of grief. Be sad. Be sad for a long time. This grief is **not** sick. I will not pathologize your grief.

Grief is brutal. It hurts. And the intensity of grief can be powerfully intense for you if you have recently lost someone or something very close to you.

- Grief is exhausting. It wears a person out, and saps energy. Folks who are grieving feel like their limbs are heavy, like they can't do as much in a day, like a nap is necessary to get through the day.

- Grief affects the body in real ways. Folks who have lost someone often feel sucker punched by the physical ache that grief creates. It's true—on brain scans, the pain of grief shows up in the same way physical pain does in the brain.

- Sleep is often a huge issue in grief. It might take hours to fall asleep. Or you might wake hours before sunrise. There are many hours where the world is sleeping, and you aren't, and all you can think of is loss. It takes forever for morning to come. In the night, each sleepless, sad-filled minute seems an hour.

- There are legitimate cognitive effects. You have lower levels of concentration and decreased ability to problem solve. You are more liable to lose your keys or forget to get groceries that were on your list. You may find reading is difficult or even impossible.

North American culture acknowledges grief that accompanies the death of a close loved one. When the death of a parent, child, or spouse occurs, they allow a few days off work. People send cards and flowers. Often, they bring over a casserole or cookies to express their condolences when they come for a short visit. There is a funeral or memorial service that honors the dearly departed where people attend to pay their respects and provide support to the surviving family.

However, after the funeral, life returns to normal for just about everybody.

Our culture has little ability to acknowledge the significant impact grief has on those whose lives are forever changed by the death of a loved one.

North American culture is even worse at recognizing loss that isn't a death. Grief is such an integral part of all loss.

Loss is a part of life. We don't just grieve when loved ones die. Things leave our life. Roles we cherish end. Dreams and ideas die. Relationships are destroyed. For example, people grieve the loss of:

- Career after retirement
- A dream when they didn't get into the university program they had been working towards
- Financial stability with unexpected bankruptcy
- Marriage through divorce
- Freedom, quality sleep, independence when becoming a new parent (even when the baby is longed for and delighted in)
- A body part after an accident, or a house through fire, or a first apartment when you move into a house

Loss creates grieving. It is a normal, natural response to loss.

Grieving is the consequence of losing someone or something or even an idea you love.

Great love inspires great grief.

And grief generally lasts. In our instant culture, we take pain killers for headaches, and antacids for a stomach ache. When we are hungry, we make microwave popcorn in 2 minutes, and pop in a pizza pocket for an instant lunch. There is an inconvenient side to grief—it doesn't subside quickly. There is nothing quick about grief.

Normal grief is hard. But it resolves with support of friends and grieving in the way that makes sense for the person grieving. Some need to cry every day. Some feel the urge to talk about the loss frequently. Others need to return to routine quickly, while others stop and process the loss deliberately while stopping activities for a time.

Everybody needs the support of others during grief. However, what that support looks like varies from person to person.

I thought I wouldn't make it through the loss of Branden and Matthew. It seemed, with no exaggeration, that insanity was a very distinct possibility.

But it didn't kill me. And, in fact, I moved through the very initial intense grief to learning to live with it as a part of me. Slowly. Over a long time.

My brother and wife invited us to sit on their back deck that first Father's Day afternoon when we were beside ourselves.

People who loved us send us cards. I valued those cards and the notes they held like I value breathing.

Friends dropped by and took me out for lunch. I suspect I wasn't pleasant company, but they didn't seem to mind. They loved me anyway.

My husband-at-the-time held me every night while I cried.

And I woke up every morning. One plodding, leaden foot in front of the other.

Day after day.

After a couple of months, with much prodding, my husband convinced me to send out my resume. I nearly wept at the interview when Patti asked me why I wanted this job. I remember smiling a plastic smile, saying all the correct things that a person is supposed to say about why they want to work at a position, when inside I felt like I was screaming: "I don't want this #&@*$ job, I want to be at home with my babies!"

But I started the position about 3 months after they died. I went for coffee with my colleagues at the start of each shift. I worked with patients in the out-patient clinic. I developed the program, with policies and patterns, and developed a referral base. I did it because they were paying me to do it. I did assessments and treatments and got to know interesting people and laughed with them to help them feel comfortable. I went through the motions of a meaningful existence.

After a while, I noticed that I now laughed because I was finding humor in my life again. I still wept, but it went from feeling as if the loss defined me, to gradually being *one* of the things that defined me. It moved from *dominating* my life, to being *something in* my life. Inch by inch, I began engaging in my life because it felt meaningful again.

My grief isn't "done", but it's become a part of me. I wouldn't have it any other way. Slowly, almost imperceptibly, grief moved from the principal feeling to one of many feelings.

I have two little clay statues in my living room now with Branden and Matthew's names stamped in the back of the figurines across the overalls. Two little birds sitting on a branch hanging in my kitchen. Their teddy bear tucked on the top shelf in the bedroom's corner facing out into the room. A small painting of two birds on a branch in the bathroom. These little guys have a place in my home.

These first sons of mine are still a part of my life, but rather than being solely a source of pain, their memory has carved me into being kinder and gentler. As a person who has known profound loss, I'm not terrified of it. I don't avoid people after they lose something and are sad. I'm grateful for who these boys were in my life.

If your grief is normal, which means agonizing, distressing, exhausting and painful, then you may not need to see a therapist. You may merely need to gather your people around you in a way meaningful for you. Let them hug you and hand you tissues. Teach them when you need them to listen to your stories. Tell them when you need them to distract you with something to give you a break from your own thoughts. Let them know when you need to pull away to cry, write, and be in solitude.

Rinse and repeat.

Your grief may become complex and require professional support. You may get stuck and the people around you don't know what to do. But that's for another chapter.

Most likely, faced with loss, **you need your people**. You need space and permission to grieve.

And you need to be painfully and naturally very sad.

Because that's what grief does.

And there's nothing wrong with that.

5 You are moving through with healthy coping

I meet with Mary every Thursday morning for coffee for just over an hour. We've done this for about 14 years. We started meeting when my husband-at-the-time was in the process of leaving our marriage.

We were both hurting—Mary and he were co-pastors of a new little church. Mary and I both felt abandoned, albeit in very different ways. I fondly called her "the other woman in his life". After multiple years of an effective close working relationship, he was leaving her as a respected colleague as well.

We met initially to go for a walk—as a support to each other. It felt valuable, and so we met again. It wasn't long before we were meeting once a week for coffee. A little support group—as we grieved his painful behavior and then departure. We swapped stories, and when we felt confused, it was reassuring to know the other was confused too. When something made little sense to her, she would check with me, and I could confirm that it didn't make sense to me either.

We could be there for each other—I heard her pain, she heard mine. We supported each other as we labored through the pain of being left behind. We understood each other in a situation we didn't understand.

During those early days, I went to see a therapist a few times. He was invaluable. But as the months went on, and the therapist moved to a different position, and phased that part of his practice out, I was left without a therapist. And that was OK.

It worked to not have him as a therapist because Mary and I still met for coffee. Every week, we have met at about 8:15 am on Thursday for coffee for about 90 minutes. When I was working sixty hours a week at two jobs,

I still made time. Early on, money was tight, and although a latte wasn't in the budget, the expense of the plain tea was always a priority.

Over the years, sometimes she has a workshop she is leading out of town on a Thursday morning—so we don't meet that week. Once we stopped for 3 months because she was on sabbatical. Sometimes, I have had to teach a class or a seminar on that morning. And when either of us goes on vacation, we don't meet either.

But unless one of us has a commitment that we have let the other know about, we meet. If we haven't talked about cancelling, we're there. If I'm not sure if she has cancelled, I go—and same with her. Meeting at Starbucks at 8:15 on Thursdays is our default.

We now rarely see each other outside of Thursday mornings—maybe twice a year. We hardly call or text either during the week. But Thursday mornings find us slipping immediately into the easy, friendly and familiar camaraderie that is our rhythm.

When I was more tired this winter than usual, she held me accountable to go to the doctor. She reminded me of the energy it takes to be part of a two-families-who-are-also-one-family situation, where I am parenting children that are not my biological children. Mary challenged me on my schedule and asked about some decisions I had made that left me over committed. She asked me why I was saying, "yes" to so many things. Mary wouldn't let me get away with any stock answers. She expected me to be candid with her and dug until we got to the root of it. It's a profound thing to have someone in our lives who can call us on our sh*t!

Mary is good for me. I like to think I am good for her.

Mary has an aging mother to whom she is completely devoted. She has ensured her mother receives excellent care all day every day. Her brothers are out of town, so, as the only child of her very elderly mom in the city, she takes her to all her appointments. She worries about her. Her mother, with memory failing her in the last months, has taken to calling Mary many times a day seeking reassurance. Mary and I have had some candid conversations about the level of care her mom requires. We wonder out loud how much to aggressively fight every health issue her mom has, and how Mary can prepare herself for the inevitable death of her mother.

These haven't always been easy discussions, but they are very real. We don't avoid topics to be polite. We have invested so much into this relationship and have so much trust between each other. I give her significant latitude to poke and prod into the vulnerable areas of my life. We have a significant level of transparency between each other. She is going to hear about the rough spots of my life as they happen.

Sometimes she supports me and reminds me about my strengths and why she loves me when I am too hard on myself. Other times, she gently chides me when she hears me being judgemental. She gets curious when I'm upset and doesn't let me just sit and stew about it. Sometimes, I get all up in my head, and things get twisted up tight—and she lets me talk. As I rant in bits and chunks, she takes the pieces and helps me make sense of them.

She isn't a therapist, and she doesn't expect me to be hers. But we have a level of accountability that allows for support, care, challenge and nurture when we hit rough spots of life. Regardless of when hard stuff happens, Thursday is coming. We will have a candid conversation about it. We also have someone who is a cheerleader and I know that I can celebrate accomplishments with her—I know she won't perceive it as bragging. She will, more than most, appreciate all the bumps and barriers I had to tackle to allow for the achievement.

I have other friends, too, who prompt my growth, and support me in challenges. My friend, Judy, is a brave soul. Some might consider her somewhat outspoken. I just consider her a friend.

I just see her as courageously honest. Being Judy's friend is a *little* risky and a **lot** wonderful. She is an extrovert who embraces life. It gives her a wide circle of friends. I noticed that her boldness gives her more opportunity to be kind. She's not afraid to call someone up who might need help.

Judy and I took a trip to Chicago several years ago to see Oprah Winfrey talk to Brené Brown as part of a taping of some episodes of *Oprah's Lifeclass*.

I offered to hang around Chicago airport for a few hours to wait for Judy's arrival on a later flight so we could take the train downtown together.

Judy forbade me to wait.

She insisted I get on the train from the airport and start exploring the city without her. When Judy talks, I take her seriously. It meant this timid soul of mine found out it was quite capable of negotiating the train in Chicago. I saw parts of downtown I would have missed if I'd quietly waited for her at the airport, as would have been my natural bent.

She traded shifts at work to come to Chicago with me. She's a nurse. It shouldn't be possible in August on 3 weeks' notice amid a beautiful and short Canadian summer to get the time—but Judy pulled it off. She trades favors with people *like nobody's business*. She makes things happen, calling in favors with all those she has generously helped out in the past.

When we were deciding what to do on our free evening the day before the show taping, we put our heads together in the hotel lobby. We tossed out ideas, realized which ones weren't possible because of the time of day, and determining which ones piqued both of our interest. We both love theatre, and she noticed a play that she'd heard was great was having a show nearby. I had just seen on ads on most light poles in downtown Chicago as the play to see. I was in!

Carolyn, the introvert, looks for theatre tickets in the way most natural to her—I *quietly googled* for tickets. This was an unexpected, unbudgeted trip for each of us, so we were on the hunt for discounts. I found tickets for $90—third balcony. A chunk of change certainly, but we were in Chicago, after all—should we just go for it?

Judy looked for tickets in *her* way. She found someone and asked. When she went off to get us each a drink in the hotel lobby, she didn't return for a long time. When she did get back, she let me know about her "new best friend, Anthony", a hotel staffer who knows stuff about Chicago. She had asked him what the best approach to get tickets was.

Her newest friend, Anthony, told her how to get tickets for $25. Yep, twenty-five bucks! And **not** nosebleed seats either. We followed Anthony's instructions by racing over to the theatre and hanging out in the lobby to get the last-minute unsold great seats.

We sat in the 10th row in a huge theatre with three balconies! Those seats put us back $25 even—not a single extra fee. The guy beside us paid ten times that for his ticket. The play was hilarious, and had great songs with tight harmonies, and dancing that took my breath away.

I'd been working that summer on being more confident in unfamiliar situations. Judy taught me more on that trip than I'd learned all summer.

Hanging out with her in Chicago was worth 10 therapy sessions to witness, experience and practice courage and self confidence in strange circumstances!

Many of us are fortunate to have people in our lives supportive to us when the going gets rough. When we have life circumstances or life goals we need to work through, some of us are able to do that task because we have people around us. The community provides us with an environment in which we can grow and thrive.

Not everybody does.

Maybe you have people to whom you can show your wounded parts, and they cradle those parts. Do you have people who can challenge you when they see you mess up? And as they do, they do it in a way that leaves you feeling like they just love you so much that they want you to be a better person?

Then perhaps you don't need a therapist for the situation you are facing.

Do you have people in your life who don't let you be content with who you are now, and they love you enough to push you to improve yourself? And you trust them to make you uncomfortable because you know it's good for you?

If you have a caring tribe around you who can challenge and support and nurture you towards being more fully who you are, then you may not need counseling. You need loving folk who call you back to the beautiful core of you. Some need to have a professional play this role in our lives. If you have people in your life that can lovingly confront you in such a way that you say respond with both, "Ouch" and, "Thank you", consider yourself blessed.

If you have a person with whom who you feel safe to tell them how scared you are, and they respect you and tell you they are grateful for how you were brave to tell them, then you may be fortunate enough to have the sufficient resources to guide you through the struggle of life.

If you have solid people who are good for you and there for you, then you may be able to do the work you need to do when you hit a rough spot in life without a therapist.

6 You are not in a place ready to do the work

I've always admired split-second timing.

For example:

- When the batter hits a home run.

  It's magic when the bat connected with the ball at precisely the right position at the right time to propel it over the fence. The ball needs to connect with the bat at the exact precise instance. Too early or too late will make a foul ball. Hit true and far, it sails over the outfield into the stands.

- Great comedy is far more than fantastic jokes.

  Legendary comedians know how to time their delivery razor sharpness to impact the humor level of the material. We often celebrate comedians for having "good timing".

- Cheerleaders who move in formation as together they chant and dance are amazing.

  As some boost others up and flip them through the air, still others arrive in position to catch them perfectly. If they aren't there at the precise moment—ouch!

Timing is critical in so many situations, isn't it?

Several years ago, I remember a therapist colleague walking into the office. She had a full afternoon and evening booked with clients. Just on her way over to the office, she had discovered that her brother had died. He was elderly and had been sick, but his death had been sudden.

She was reeling—and her first client of the day was already in the waiting room, waiting for the appointment to begin.

She stumbled into my office, almost in a daze. She gave me the news of the family death and wondered out loud about the day. Her brother lived in Europe and she was powerless to do anything that day. She was certain she wanted to proceed with the therapy sessions.

Therapists understand that a client's time is valuable and often there has been a significant lead-up of emotional planning and energy required prior to an appointment. Sometimes, people don't sleep well the night prior to an appointment. They can spend the hours prior to the appointment trying to decide how to talk about something important, or just even dreading the idea of bringing it up. Other times, clients have been eagerly awaiting the time to talk with someone they trust, and who facilitates them to move forward. Clients are often excited to anticipate sharing exciting progress or ways in which they have created a shift in their lives.

The therapists I know are committed to keeping the appointments they have made with clients, because they are cognizant that cancelling at the last minute can be so disappointing for a client. Cancelling at the last minute might mean that we aren't able to reach the client prior to them leaving their home or work for the appointment—and it can be brutal for anyone to get to an appointment only to find it cancelled. Arriving at a therapy appointment only to find it cancelled can be disheartening.

The news of her brother's death overwhelmed my colleague and now she had the challenge of a full day of clients beginning almost immediately.

Making a split-second decision, knowing her determination and commitment to her clients, I made the choice to say something like this:

"Normally, I would say how sorry I am, and would spend some time listening and asking questions about your loss—but I don't think that would be kind, given your choice to see clients today. So, I won't hug you as I would normally hug a friend in your position because now is the time to focus on the day ahead. Right now, it's time to get your head in this game. You want to see clients today so that's the focus right now. Let's go turn on the lights in your office. Let's go get you settled into your room."

I used a calm, business-like tone, not the softer tone I felt pulled to use when someone I care about has lost someone they care about. I kept my distance from her and stayed formal.

She wanted to be ready to see clients in a few minutes, and embracing her, being empathic and consoling would be to elicit the grief at a time that wasn't appropriate for her.

She would not ignore her brother's death in the big picture. But she was committed to doing what she felt was the right thing to do that day. So I helped her postpone the beginning of her grief until there was time and space to weep.

I was not unkind to her that day in my brisk-ish tone. My intention was quite the opposite. She had chosen a job to do, and my intention was to help her postpone her grieving for a day to help her to do it. I knew there would be time later to mourn and contemplate his life and grieve his death when she could sink into her feelings.

It actually felt as though it would have been unkind to be soft and soothing, giving her a warm hug and asking her to talk about her brother. To provide a conversation where she would have burst into sobbing minutes before focusing on a client would have been most unkind.

Timing is important in counseling. Sometimes those around you advise you to get help, but you're not ready.

For some people who aren't ready, there are short-term issues:

- A college student goes on a first date, set up by her friends. Her date is rude to the server and talks about himself at length all evening. He is insensitive and doesn't really engage her in conversation. She excuses herself to walk home alone and finds herself crying. She is oddly but significantly upset by sitting at the table with this man for an evening. She has trouble sleeping that night, with painful moments of the evening playing through her head. She has never reacted this way before. She wants to process her reaction to the date. Her friends in psychology wonder if it's "daddy issues", which is possible, given her father's relationship with her. However, it is 10 days before exams. Her friends suggest that she put her experience of the date and the reaction that followed on the back burner to focus on studies. She makes an appointment to see a therapist after her semester is over.

For others, the issues are bigger and longer term:

- A man comes in for assistance in grieving the sudden death of his wife in a motor vehicle accident and asks for help in therapy to parent his teen-aged daughters as they also grieve. He speaks longingly and lovingly of his wife, missing her terribly. He grieves the end of their marriage. One session he grieves how he wasn't the husband he would have wanted to be for her. He's tortured that he worked too much, was too distracted with his own interests and so on. He wonders if he was a disappointment to her. He does not return for another appointment. No explanation provided. Two years later, he returns. After some friendly chitchat about the intervening two years, he discloses to the therapist that early in his marriage she had a one-night stand with a man while on a business trip. She kept this information from him as a secret for two decades. He discovered the infidelity in some letters after her death. He tells the therapist he had to stop coming two years prior, because he wasn't ready to disclose this secret to anyone at that point. He told the therapist he needed to focus on raising his daughters, which had become suddenly very challenging because his wife, and their mom had died. He was experiencing an intense shift in his life with the death of his wife, missing her and adjusting to life without her. His shock over the long-ago-infidelity stayed on the back burner. He was certain that if he had also disclosed her infidelity, he would have drowned in the pain. He wanted to just miss her *then*—**now** he was ready to deal with his anger. The intensity of adjustment, loss, sadness and loneliness of the time had now subsided. He was now able to look at her actions all those years ago. He had now returned, feeling ready and able to deal with his intense shame and anger that arose as a result of his wife's actions all those years ago.

There are times when the current circumstances suggest that it makes little sense to deal with more. Where going about your day to get life done, following routines, or dealing with the crises at hand is what makes sense.

The additional processing of therapy may lead to feelings, which, in that moment, are not the right time to feel.

It's all about the timing.

‏‮ℰℰ‬‎

Please recognize that there are categorical differences to "not being in a spot ready to do the work because of timing" vs "I don't really want to do the work at all." These are two vastly different situations. However, people often pass the latter off as the former:

- I can't deal with our marriage now because I have a huge project at work that demands my full attention. Don't ask me to go to therapy when I'm up for the big promotion at work and they are looking to see how I handle this project.
  - o This may be a timing issue if this is a one-time big endeavor. However, often this is the latest huge project after many years of big projects. It may be that this approach to a job is part of what has caused the marriage to crumble.
- I can't deal with my drinking right now because of our daughter's upcoming wedding. There are a million details to plan, and so many parties as a part of this event where alcohol will be served. The alcohol is part of celebrating our daughter's marriage. I can't focus on my drinking when this is such a good time of our lives. I don't want to take any focus off my daughter's joy.
  - o This sounds like a timing issue, at first blush. But in reality, it is also a time of celebration of marriage and of grieving the loss of a certain relationship with her as formally

begins her own family of two. Precisely the occasions that often exacerbate excessive drinking habits. There is never a perfect moment to address excessive substance abuse. It's safe to say that when family is challenging you on excessive drinking, it has already become a real problem for them. It's likely that if you're being encouraged to deal with your alcohol consumption now, it's because a family member—maybe even your daughter—is worried that your drinking. There is likely concern that the most celebrated moments of her life will be negatively impacted.

- Yes, I had a difficult childhood that was abusive. Yes, those foster homes shuffled me around and I never felt part of a family. Yes, those years of partying to cope with the pain of my childhood were destructive. But that's all gone, I'm fine now. I'm just barely finally enjoying my life, my job, my husband, and my kids. I don't want to rock the boat now when I finally look like I have it together.

  o This may be a valid claim. It's can be helpful to delay the start of therapy until after a period of sustained stability. Therapy can feel destabilizing. Starting the work of counseling from a position of strength can be helpful. However, it is possible that this desire not to rock the boat is ignoring the nightmares that leave her exhausted in the morning. Or it may mean the unwillingness to challenge her husband on even simple everyday matters that keeps them from being as close as they would be otherwise. It could be that this "stability" is only achieved by unsustainable behaviors like incessant cleaning, cooking, ironing and attending to every detail all the time in a way that is exhausting. This may not be an authentic, "I'm in a good place now" statement, but something said desperately, with teeth gritted behind a façade of peace.

⋦⋩⋫

The real challenge is to sort out which category your desire not to attend therapy belongs.

- Is it a real reason?
- Is it an empty excuse?

This is important to process with integrity: Is your stated story to attend therapy a reason or an excuse?

❧❧

There are valid reasons a person should not attend therapy at this time—or at all.

Then there are excuses disguised as reasons such as throwing stories out to avoid making an appointment for therapy. Frantically, eagerly searching for any reason at all to avoid dealing with that which holds you back in life. Desperately but firmly, stating whatever is needed to ensure that you don't have to show up and face the issue which you are avoiding. Like a person in a sinking boat throwing off ballast to prevent sinking, you may throw out desperate lines when people tell you that *this* (whatever *this* is) can't continue.

Throwing out those excuses won't stop your boat from sinking.

Desperate excuses and **valid reasons** often sound similar on the outside.

They may look and sound the same in conversation.

But internally, they come from diverse places.

And teasing out the difference between an excuse and reason is what the next section is all about.

Section III Empty excuses for why people avoid counseling

If you're a parent, you know that there is a difference between a real reason and an empty excuse. If you're not a parent, let me give you an example of the difference:

Your 17-year-old comes home 2 hours late from the curfew time you had both agreed on.

- Excuse: His friend, who gave him a ride refused to leave on time, and your son's phone battery died so he couldn't call you to tell you that.
- Reason: His friend fell at the party and was bleeding profusely. Your son called the ambulance and was putting pressure on the wound. In the confusion of getting to the hospital, time got away on him and he forgot to call.

He might claim that the excuse is a reason, but as a parent, you recognize the difference, right?

You get a note from your 13-year-old son's teacher saying that she is waiting to get back last week's math test with your signature on it. It was due to be returned 3 days ago. He rotated through the following when asked about it:

- Excuse #1: He just keeps forgetting to ask his parents to sign it.
- Excuse #2: Then he tried telling the teacher his parents lost it.

- Excuse #3: Or maybe he had forgotten it in his locker.

This one happened at our house. We pushed him on it. Why did he have a whole rolodex of excuses? We wondered out loud why he generally did his assigned homework and yet did not get this done. We reminded him that the expectation of him being a student is to fulfill the requests of the teacher. We didn't let him get away with it. Eventually he gave us this reason:

- Reason: He simply didn't see the value in having his parents sign it.

We could hardly believe that—we wondered if he was ashamed of his grade. We racked our brains why this child didn't complete this task. (Although he is a great kid and almost always honest, by this time he had just given us three excuses that didn't hold water.)

Then we gave him some motivation to get the job done: We told him then until he had completed this responsibility, he would have to wash all the supper dishes all by himself every day until he located the test, got it signed and returned it to the teacher.

The excuses disappeared.

This boy who hates dishwashing more than anything in life had the test signed and returned within 24 hours. The grade was fine.

Funny what a little dishwashing motivation can do to inspire a young man to get something done. His *reasons* were really just *excuses*.

Excuses are often like that, aren't they?

If you're anything like me, it's not always easy to tell the difference between an excuse and a reason.

I've come to learn that discerning between a reason and excuses is most difficult when I'm the one who is doing the talking.

I often need to take to think and soul search to know if my rationale is valid or a rationalization that doesn't really measure up.

The best way for me to know if my statements hold water is to talk it through.

7 Therapy is for sissies

I f you believe situation comedies, a therapy session is a time when the therapist endlessly inquires, *"And how does that make you feel?"*

Then clients have endless permission to indulge themselves in self-pity as they sob about all the terrible things that have happened to them. (All this therapy happens while a client lies on a chaise of some sort, as they lean on one end, lying on their back with their feet stretched out on the far side.) The stereotype seems to imply that those who attend therapy are helpless victims and all therapy will reinforce this helplessness.

For the record, I have a personal policy to **never** ask a client, "And how does that make you feel?" (Though, for the record, we have a chaise in one of our offices. To my knowledge, a client has never stretched out on it, *sit com* style.)

Modern culture would have us believe that spineless folks go to be indulged by therapists: "There, there. You poor, poor dear".

It bears exploring: Is therapy for sissies?

Our North American culture places a high value on people solving their own problems, creating their own destiny, and doing it on their own *every* step of the way.

We would prefer to think we are always in control of our own choices and that we only do what we *consciously* decide to do. We believe if we decide to do or utter something, or to not do or express something, that if we have our act together, we will just live in line with our choices. We will just do what we recognize is best.

Really?

Do you always do what you decide? Do your decisions always come from a reasoned, rational place that considers what is in your best interests and the best interests of the loved ones around you?

⋘⋙

Join me in thinking about a few questions:

Do you ever eat more than you should, or eat foods you regret later on? In other words, do you ever emotionally eat?

Are you in relationships that aren't functioning effectively, and yet, you say nothing?

Do you ever:

- gamble more than you intend
- drink more than you've decided
- spend more than you've budgeted for, or
- spend hours longer on social media than you've planned?

Do you unintentionally numb yourself in ways that prevent you from engaging fully in your own life?

Do you ever decide about how you will handle a difficult situation with your boss, or your child, or your mother—and then don't follow through with it? Oh, you can make some excuses about why it didn't work—but you don't end up having the conversation that you think needs having.

Do you ever:

- Decide not to apply for the promotion, or not to ask her out on a date, so you can avoid the disappointment if it doesn't work out?
- Act so goofy when you want to ask your spouse about the out-of-control budget he doesn't take you seriously?
- Speak so quietly he can't possibly hear you?
- Find yourself too busy to figure out how to get to the party?
- Not try too hard on the mixed softball team you play on—so you don't risk as much when it doesn't turn out as you'd hoped?

Did you ever say something in a stronger, meaner manner than how you intended? Did you ever get mean and say nasty things to someone you care about? Did you ever crush someone with words or fists and regret it?

Now—what kind of courage would it require to acknowledge to a therapist the ugly, candid truth about one of these questions?

Can a sissy own up to eating or spending too much? Can a weakling acknowledge that they didn't go all out in pursuit of their goals? Can a wuss speak out loud that they watch themselves behaving in the relationship in ways that sabotage the very love that they seek?

In a word, **no**.

Speaking out vulnerably is courageous.

Evidently, North American culture has never born witness to a counseling session in my office. There is nothing wimpy about coming in and saying, "I have a problem with ______ and because of this, I find myself creating problems for myself and others. I want to deal with it."

That is vulnerable for sure.

It's definitely not something a sissy would say.

It's brave and bold.

It's tackling an issue head on.

Since when do "tackling an issue head on" and "sissy" belong in the same sentence?

Answer: **They don't.**

Therapy is hard and risky work. It is not for the faint of heart.

Counseling works with people to go to utter things out loud that haven't seen the light of day for years—or maybe ever.

Saying the painful realities out loud makes them real.

Staying away from therapy and letting your fearsome realities remain unspoken allows them to exist in some twilight zone. That twilight zone allows you to move forward in life as if they don't exist, even as the foundations of what is important to you erodes by passive neglect.

Let me give you a few examples that can only be defined as courageous, of what brings people to therapy:

- **Acknowledging responsibility for your role in your marriage as it slowly deteriorates.**

It is infinitely easier to blame your spouse for causing all the problems than to speak your heartbreak to a therapist. To wonder aloud where it went wrong, and if there is any action you may have taken part in the patterns that had you get off track—that is **not** the easy way out.

It is far easier to become absorbed in your career or your kids so you are too busy to feel the pain of the distance of your relationship. Being preoccupied is a great way to pretend nothing's wrong—even as the foundation of your marriage continues to erode.

- **Expressing discomfort about troublesome relationships you have with your child, or maybe your parent.**

Starting that conversation with a therapist means you can't fake that the discomfort doesn't exist anymore. And when you acknowledge it to be true, the ball starts rolling and we don't know what it looks like when it reaches bottom.

It may mean that eventually, you may even talk about it with your mother, or with your son.

If starting that ball rolling isn't courage, then what is?

- **Being real about how fears that have developed from the ghosts of traumas past continue to pull the strings in your life.**

Facing the effects of past trauma is terrifying. I have sat with many clients who have disclosed the pain of sexual violation; the loss of a parent, a career of public protection; or been a veteran of war, or a social worker who feels like she is still on the front lines of a war. Folks who have seen and felt things that can't be unseen and unfelt.

If you are a survivor of trauma, you understand how a life is spent avoiding the nightmares, the anxiety, certain intersections, locations, positions, songs, times of day. You dodge anything that might trigger the body into forgetting that the memory is only a memory. Trust me, when these folks walk into a therapy room, wanting to address the chokehold the trauma has on their lives, their photo is beside the word "courage" in my dictionary.

"Sissy" and *"going to therapy"* don't belong in the same sentence.

- **Going beneath the anger to acknowledge the fear, or be real about the loss, or to feel the hurt.**

It's not courageous to be angry when your girlfriend breaks up with you, or you don't get into that course, your wife gets a cancer diagnosis, or your doctor says your body will never be able to have children. It's *natural*, but it's not courageous. It's just normal.

It's tempting to stay mad. It's easier to stay mad.

Being mad is a strategy to stay away from the feelings that are inevitably underneath the anger. These emotions have us feel fragile—and everything in us (and I include myself in "us") wants to run away from the feelings. Underneath the anger of not getting into the course is the unspoken fear of, "What will I do if I don't do this? And if I'm not good enough to get into that course, am I not good enough, period?" Underneath the anger towards cancer is the fear of single parenting, and the potential unspeakable and unfathomable grief of losing a spouse. Underneath the anger is often a feeling of deep inadequacy.

Getting angry is normal.

Staying angry is easy.

Digging underneath the anger in a curious and honest way is courageously vulnerable. Delving underneath the anger allows a person to deal with the fears, the potential grief, the guilt, the injustice, the fatigue, the resentment, or whatever is underneath.

- **Acknowledging the use of old patterns that worked well when you were younger, but now pull you out of your authenticity.**

I talked with a friend the other day who spent years in a bad marriage. Her husband travelled a lot on business—and it worked in her favour that he was gone more than he was at home. When he was at home, she would grit her teeth, and wait it out. She would endure his time at home until he would leave again.

The marriage ended, and after a time, she fell in love. She remarried and now delights that her now-husband comes home at the end of every workday. He has two sons who live with them half time. As she and his sons are working out their relationship, there are inevitable rough spots. It is normal that as two families combine to also become one family, there are some tensions.

She recently found herself steeling herself for the few days these children are at their house until they return to be with their mother.

When she noticed the "steeling herself", she caught herself. She was behaving towards them now the way she used to respond to her husband back then. She was taken aback when she noticed it. Transposing the reality of a bad marriage onto a new relationship with stepchildren would not be helpful. Confronting that feeling and admitting was brave and insightful, I think.

It's likely that she and these children can negotiate a friendly, if not fantastic relationship, but only if she can pull herself out of that pattern that she almost inevitably finds herself returning to. There's a part of her that knows these children are not her ex-husband in a bad marriage, even as another part automatically treats these children like part time frustrating family member she must endure. She wants them to be full-time children of her heart—and that will only happen if she can break the pattern. And she can only break the pattern if she works through it.

You have to know that if you show up in my therapy office we see you as a person who is strong and courageous because you are willing to look at the hardest parts of your life.

Folks who choose to go to counseling are wise investors.

58

Clients come to therapy willing to do hard things because they believe that the healing inside themselves and in their relationships will be a payoff that is well worth it.

Quite simply, therapy is hard and risky work.

8 Therapy is intimidating

When I went to grad school for my counseling degree, it was expected that as part of the process I would do my own personal work in therapy. To counselor-in-training was expected to see her own counselor. This was for two reasons:

1. If therapists are going to work with clients on a client's stuff, they need to know what's it's like to work through their own stuff. It's only fair that therapists feel a pounding heart thump in their chest as they wait for the first session, uncertain of how the session will go, right? Therapists need to understand what it is like to be a client. Clients deserve the compassion and understanding of a therapist who truly gets it. And I believe therapists, taking part as clients, need to experience a session when the therapist doesn't understand them or is insensitive to themselves as the client. When their therapist doesn't quite get it, is judgemental or is pushing hard unrealistically—therapists have to know what that feels like as a client. Therapists need to experience therapy from the perspective of a client to better understand what their clients are experiencing.

2. Therapists are flawed human beings. Don't you want them to have worked on their stuff before they help you with yours? That's no surprise, because none of us is perfect. No therapist will have "arrived" at complete personal enlightenment, but don't you want them on their own journey towards wholeness? Every therapist will have unique perspectives because of who they are and their own personal life experiences. I also believe that one factor that makes for a good therapist is recognizing their own humanity, in its authentic imperfectness. As therapists, we have a professional and personal obligation to deal with our stuff.

Counselors need to become aware of their biases and blind spots to reduce the likelihood that we will impose them on our clients. We need to deal with our own trauma and our own vulnerability so we don't ask our clients to do something we don't know how to do ourselves. And we need to have worked through that which scares us as humans—because some of our clients and some issues that arise in therapy can be hard to hear. Counselors need to know how to deal with their own internal world so it won't stop them as they take the client through therapy. Good therapists know what triggers their own issues, and that awareness helps us prevent our stuff interfering with your stuff as you come in to talk about it.

I found myself making all sorts of excuses when it was the time in my counseling education to do the research to find a therapist who sees therapists and make the call to make the appointment. I told myself I would call after breakfast, or after doing that school reading for my next class, or after I put the kids down for their nap. Before I knew it, business hours had passed and I wouldn't be able to call until the next day. There was always a reason to postpone the call. This went on for a week or more.

You know why I didn't really call. I realized it, too, but it was hard to admit at the moment:

I was scared.

Plain and simple, the idea of going to a therapist was frightening. I'm a person who invests fully in my plans and decisions, and so I had no plans to *go through the motions* with a therapist. I wouldn't *pretend* to do therapy—I was going to be all in. That idea of doing therapy—exposing myself fully to a therapist—then, was terrifying

To go to therapy was to open myself up to someone who was, before I started therapy, a total stranger. This total-stranger-therapist had permission, because of his role, to respond however he liked. The normal constraints of most conversations where we instinctively know and operate out of the belief that personal stuff is *none of your business* wouldn't exist.

We know in conventional conversations that people won't ask pointed questions that will make the conversation awkward. Social courtesy won't push for further explanation that which was intentionally left unsaid. A therapist doesn't have those limitations.

It's the job of therapists to go to those unsaid places, because that's often where the pain is, and therefore, where the healing is.

The therapist would expect me to expose my problems. It makes sense that we would spend most of the time on the trouble spots of my thinking and feeling. It was to be expected that important experiences that were painful would come up.

I would be walking into the room expecting the therapist to scrutinize things I hadn't explored yet; help me process pain that I had thus far avoided; and open up to being exposed to blind spots that might embarrass me.

What I *expected* the therapist to do was also *precisely* what freaked me out.

I didn't want to admit that I feared being a therapy client. But I did. I was already seeing clients as a therapist, and I had normalized their anxiety—but was having a hard time overcoming my own.

The great part about grad school, and semesters, and graduation is that I could only procrastinate for a short period. Everything is on a timeline. Eventually, the motivation to graduate became stronger than the fear of going to counseling.

After a long winter, it's garden season. I do not have a green thumb.

I worked hard on my flower beds one weekend spring day. We had a lot of rain the previous couple of days, and there was a brief break on the weekend with beautiful sunshine before several more forecasted days of rain. It seemed that planting now would give the baby plants a good soak immediately after they got planted.

I'd put off the spring gardening for a while. Some delay was because of schedule—and some of it due to bugs. I **hate** bugs. I avoid bugs, and activities that provide exposure to bugs. But I do like flowers—even more than I hate bugs. I took a deep breath, put on garden gloves to create a barrier between the bugs and I, and launched into the weeding, and preparing the earth.

As I was gardening, the process reminded me of the work I do as a therapist. Actually, the original logo of my private practice was that of a seed in the dirt.

Picture being a seed planted in the spring. The seed is planted in the dirt and promptly doused with water. To grow, a seed needs to crack open to let new life out. To be a seed in the cold wet mud would be an uncomfortable, painful, and broken place to be—and yet ironically, are ideal conditions for growth. Who would want to be a seed in those circumstances?

And yet who wouldn't want to be a seed that becomes a beautiful plant, with colorful blooms and strong green leaves?

The years of working with clients have taught me how very difficult it is to be in painful situations. Yet that pain is often the catalyst to confront things that have been "under the radar" inside of a person and not explored. A richness and healing comes that wasn't a possibility before. It's terrifying to contemplate the unknown conversations that will happen in therapy. But it is those conversations that will create shifts inside of you that will allow for change and growth.

❧❧

I lack a green thumb. The northern location where I live in Canada which creates a shorter season doesn't actually permit me to plant seeds in the garden that will grow into flowering plants for me to enjoy. Those factors combine to have me purchase baby flowering plants local gardening nursery to plant in my flower beds

As I was planting the flowers this weekend, I was faced with a tough choice. I have a friend, Doreen, who has awesome success with planting a garden fit for a queen. She also plants bedding plants instead of seeds to lengthen the time she can enjoy the flowers on the plants. Doreen has told me how she, after planting all the flowers—she pinches off every last little bloom on the baby plants.

OUCH!!

That hurts just typing it.

It's counterintuitive really—to plant flowering plants because of the desire to see the beautiful blooms, and the moment they are first planted, to take every flowering bit and nip it off.

I think it's just wrong.

I dislike plucking flowers off of flowering plants more than I dislike bugs. And trust me, that is saying a lot!

But she does this bloom-plucking as part of a bigger plan. Doreen told me when she plucks off the first flowers, it allows energy that would normally go into those first flowers to go instead into developing the root system. It also encourages growth of more little branches and stems. Plants that have those first flowers plucked off when planted end up with fuller, bushier plants that bear more flowers. In the big picture, pinching those early blooms off the plant is worth it. The flowering plant will be fuller and brighter and more beautiful throughout the season.

To be honest, after a long winter, with months of white snow, bare branches and dirty, grey roads outside, my eyes are starved for color. Pinching those first beautiful purple, pink and yellow flowers is something that goes against everything in me. So, when I planted the plants, I debated.

To pluck or not to pluck—that was the question.

I didn't want to pluck off flowers. To pinch off beauty seemed unnecessarily harsh. It sounded wrong to harm the plant, and to do what seemed like damage to it.

But I did it. I took a deep breath (each time) and I pinched those little beautiful babies off. (OK, I kept a few tiny buds on, rationalizing they didn't count.)

❧❧

It reminded me of the courage of clients who come to see me, wanting and prepared to grow. Generally, it is some discomfort or pain that brings people into therapy:

- the pain of anxiety or depression
- a conflicted marriage
- a lost promotion
- being dumped by a girlfriend

Those situations are like the cold, wet, uncomfortable and painful soil. These people come to therapy for relief from the destructive muddy ruts they find themselves in, looking for solace and comfort with a therapist.

Yet, many of them, in the process of exploring and discussing the different layers of their inner experience, find themselves feeling like the blossoms are being plucked.

And guess who the bloom-plucking gardener is?

Me. Yours truly. The therapist.

For the record, *I take no delight* in people experiencing pain in the counseling room. It is hard to watch. It is painful as clients and I collectively take a deep breath and look at something from a unique angle to gain a better understanding. Doing so creates an experience that stings in that minute of the session. To make a previously buried hurt come alive in that moment is powerful—and acutely painful.

Sometimes, it would seem less painful in that moment to live an unexplored, unexamined life. It's easier to blame others. It hurts to honestly see one's unique role in perpetuating a painful cycle. It's easier to just be angry. When the reason for that *mad* is actually an underlying huge *sad*, it is difficult to acknowledge the deeper reality. The more powerful, more in control feeling is the surface anger—and to slow down to feel the more vulnerable, deeper feelings is a challenge that is daunting.

It hurts to be vulnerable. It's risky to share with your spouse that which is true and real but has been hidden from a spouse—not even because they are so awful, but because it's scary to be so very open. Those risk-taking events of being fully candid with your spouse are bloom-plucking experiences if there ever were any!

If you contemplate counseling, I'll be honest with this: It stings to leave a session sometimes. It doesn't always create instant rewarding feelings to gain a new level of understanding of something that you have avoided for a long time. When counseling is supposed to "make you feel better", and you leave a session feeling worse because:

- you are aware of the patterns in which you have been actively participating
- you notice for the first time how much you have allowed others to violate your boundaries
- you've allowed yourself the depth of the pain behind a betrayal, rather than just feeling the rage

—well, it can feel awful.

Yuck.

Please be aware that I, and many I've spoken to in my profession over the years, well—we admire the courage a client has to do this work.

I honor the chutzpah that you will have in being willing to risk with me as a therapist—and I don't take that honor lightly.

I know about how sometimes, in the short term, therapy hurts. However, I don't shy away from this, and will continue to walk with you into dark, tender, achy places—because I have walked this road with other people. I believe it to be a profoundly worthwhile endeavor in the big picture.

Simply put, the discoveries, the growth, and the greater healing are worth it. I know the pinching hurts. From the inside out, I get that. I make it my business to do some "first aid" to support the pain that the therapy itself can create. I seek to do the therapy work at a pace and level within tolerable limits.

But I don't avoid conversations that may cause pain-with-a-purpose.

To be unwilling to walk with you into those hard, tender spaces, would take care of my own comfort. I will not do that to you. It's an important part of honoring you to give you my best. If the wise thing to do is have an uncomfortable conversation and look at hard things with you, then I will respect you and your desire to grow. You have the right to have the very best opportunity to gain maximal benefit from therapy.

When you go to therapy, let your therapist know when something hurts. Ensure that the pain is serving a valuable purpose, and that you have resources to deal with it. Ask for help if it gets overwhelming. You may ask to slow down or take a break from something that is hard. Work with your therapist to ensure that they know how you are doing, and if a conversation is too intimidating to have at that moment. Know that your therapist is very aware of how the work of therapy itself can create pain.

An effective therapist works gently and carefully and thoughtfully, and deliberately—and with great respect. It might hurt. It might be uncomfortable and awkward. The uncertainty may be difficult. But that's part of the overall process.

I made the appointment to start my own therapy. I showed up. I invested in counseling in my style of *jump in with both feet*. And it was wonderful—but also remained a little scary throughout the process. I cried as I remembered painful things. I admitted things to my therapist about me that were painful to admit. I had conversations with my therapist that were challenging, but good.

My anxiety towards the sessions lessened over time, once I had a few sessions under my belt. I realized some ugly confrontations that that I anticipated would never happen. I soon learned my biggest fears about how he would respond to me would never occur. It wasn't his style. He wasn't out to shame me for my mistakes. He wasn't going to ridicule me. I learned that he trusted me to talk about important stuff and did far less pushing that I thought might happen.

To tell you the truth, it was *less worse* than I thought it would be. He was far kinder and more supportive than I expected. There were many times, when I was expecting him to scold me (apparently one of my issues!) and rather, he met me with compassion and curiosity. I had far more ability to influence the direction of therapy than I thought I would. It was a powerfully positive experience.

I was still a little nervous before each session, though, to be honest. That never went away.

But I think worthwhile tasks are often intimidating. I learned that it is normal to feel scared and brave in the same moment.

Can you think of a worthwhile challenge that didn't involve some risk?

Feeling scared isn't bad. It's just an honest, genuine feeling in response to a situation that normally evokes fear in most people. The dread doesn't mean you can't or shouldn't go to counseling. The fear just means that you recognize that it is an unknown.

You can name the fear to yourself, and even to your therapist. You can acknowledge it as normal and then decide how you want to honor your fear in a way that still allows you to move forward.

Being scared is, on a practical level, a very real part of the process of therapy for almost everyone.

9 The therapist will just blame my mother

No one likes the person who blames his/her problems on everybody else **but** himself:

- The professor kicked me out of the class because he didn't understand that I only cheated on a part that didn't really count for very much.

- The boss promoted Charlie ahead of me because Charlie sucks up to the boss in a way that I'm not willing to. Charlie probably stays late at work just to appear hard working for the boss.

- It's not my fault I was late and then had to speed to get to the factory on time. My mom was supposed to wake me and she didn't. She should pay for the ticket!

Blaming others looks irresponsible. Blaming others is unattractive. If you are a blamer, it's possible people will stop hanging out with you before they become a target!

My son, Carter, is a competitive volleyball player. He is an athletic guy who can jump high, move quickly, and his reflexes have to be seen to be believed. But that's not why coaches pursued him for a college team.

They pursued Carter for his character. Carter has a good heart and it shows as he works to support his fellow athletes. When they get down on themselves, he encourages them. When they make a great play, he gets visibly excited and celebrates their abilities. Starting when he was in middle school, when he made a mistake, he would raise his hand and then tap his chest, signalling, "That was my error."

A dozen universities pursued him in high school to come play for them. When I asked one university coach why he wanted to recruit my son (who at *only* 6 feet is rather short to play college ball), he said one important reason was because of how he could own his errors. It was his ability to own his own mistakes that was one quality that had university coaches saying, "Come play with us." It was his comfort in accepting responsibility for what went wrong when it was his fault that made him an attractive player. Coaches told me that other players played better when he was on the court—because he did things like own his errors. (Can you tell I'm a proud momma?)

We all admire people like my son who are comfortable enough in their own skin to admit their mistakes. These people are safe to hang around with, because we know they aren't likely to shift blame onto us for something they've done.

To own your own stuff is often admired as a quality of strength and integrity.

One of the ultimate signs of leadership is to be the one to pronounce: "I am the captain of this ship. This failure was on my watch. It's on me." That leader is one that has the back of each of his team—and people will flock to work for her/him.

So, it's no wonder then, that some avoid therapy out of the concern that the process of therapy will evolve to point fingers at others in a way that feels immature and sulky.

Who of us haven't heard lines like these?

- My therapist says my mother was so cold and distant that I continue to seek out unavailable women
- My counselor and I have decided that I drink to fill the hole that was left when my dad walked out when I was a kid·
- I can't help that I yell at my kids the way I do—I'm just parenting the way my old man parented me.

Not only is that shifting blame in a way that seems to absolve the person of responsibility, it also seems to create that person out to be a helpless victim. It's not attractive—and it creates a scene of hopelessness.

If you've read this far, promise that you'll read to the end of the chapter, even after you have read the next section.

Often in therapy, we talk about where the behaviors started. We want to explore what is underneath the feelings and thoughts.

In other words, we look for the root origin of the behaviour.

Can we agree together on a few obvious facts?

- Parents, or whoever the people were that raised us, play a pivotal role in our lives. They are the ones who held us, rocked us, fed us, diapered us. Our mothers and fathers were the ones that taught us how trustworthy our world is as our brains were just beginning to form conclusions about what the world is like. From whatever experiences you had as an infant, you learned about what the world was like. As an infant, you didn't read the papers or compare notes with your friends. You only had your own experience. When you were older, and you skinned your knee, or got left out at school, or got the flu, or got 95% (or 55%) on the test, or made (or got cut) from the team—it was your parents who reacted to what happened. Parents shape us deeply—how could they not?

- No one, not even our parents, is perfect. Wouldn't it follow then that they would have made mistakes that would affect us?

Conclusion: **Of course, our parents screwed us up**!!

And depending on your situation, you had brothers and sisters, grandparents and aunties, friends and a first crush, school yard bullies and cranky or friendly neighbors—all of whom interacted with you as you grew. You learned about what humanity was like through them. You discovered how:

- safe and reliable
- unfair or self-serving
- insecure and unpredictable
- loving and valuing your world was.

It's only a half joke amongst therapists to say that *we endeavor to raise children well enough that are able to afford their own therapy.*

⋧⋦

Note that the **chapter doesn't end here**. Therapy often does look for some root understanding of where behaviors/beliefs/understandings of the world arise. But it is not an end in itself.

Let me explain.

For a decade, I was a single mom, responsible for a household. I got the kids to their activities, made them meals, loved on them, worked two jobs to make it all happen. And I did it imperfectly. Just ask my children! They can tell you how I messed them up, despite me devoting myself to being the best mom I could be.

I still screwed up—sometimes I was too tired to do a good job of mothering, sometimes I was fearful and so I got over-protective, and other times I didn't sufficiently think things through. They are fine young adults now. I assure you they are fabulous adults, at least in some measure, *in spite* of my imperfect parenting.

Another one of the many responsibilities I had on my plate was to maintain our house. My dad is an accountant and didn't have a lot of handyman skills—and so I also have limited fix-it skills. One day, I noticed in the basement that there was a slow but steady drip coming from my ceiling in the basement and landing on a box of photographs. The box, fortunately, was plastic and so the photos were intact. I removed the stack of boxes from underneath the drip. There would be no damage to the boxes, but the drip remained. Plumbing is not in my wheelhouse, so I called John.

John was a friend of the family, and he was kind enough to be on speed dial when I was out of my league in the fix-it department. I requested him to take a gander at the leak.

He looked at the leak for several moments. I could see him tracking the pipe from where it leaked to see where it came from, and where it was going. He went upstairs and fiddled for a bit underneath the kitchen sink. He even went outside to see where the hose emerged out of the exterior wall of the house. Then he went back down to the basement to gaze at the pipe some more.

John is not a plumber either, but he eventually told me he had narrowed down the problem. He turned a tap in the ceiling I didn't even know existed, and, after a few minutes, the leak stopped.

He told me he would be back the next day with a part from the store and fix the problem. In the meantime, I shouldn't use my sink.

John puttered the next day for about a half hour with a piece of plumbing he brought with him. He turned the tap back on.

No leak.

Fixed.

John had to find the source of the problem. Not so we could stand there and point fingers and blame at the problem. John had to find the source of the problem because once he knew exactly what the problem was, he knew which piece needed replacement and repair.

John spent considerably more time finding the exact problem than he did fixing the problem. Once he knew the exact origin of the problem, the fix was actually the simple part.

That's no different from going to the doctor. If you say you have a pain in your belly, the doctor doesn't just write out a script for pain killers. He is likely to poke around in there and order some tests. Appendicitis? Bowel obstruction? Cancer? Constipation? Maybe bad gas? And is that gas from lactose intolerance, or too many beans or something else?

It makes sense to identify if the appendix or the small bowel or the liver or the kidneys are to blame for the pain. Finding the source of the pain is not the end point: "Ah, it's esophageal reflux!! I'm done. Job finished".

Rather, finding the source points towards the action plan. The specific remedy becomes obvious once there is a clear understanding of diagnosis.

Therapy works to find the deep roots of why a person does something they wish they didn't. Say, for example, a person comes to counseling wondering why she yells at her children so much. She doesn't like how angry she gets at them and worries about the damage she is inflicting on her children. Parenting well is the most important thing in her life, and she's terrified that her verbal aggression will harm her children.

Therapy explores where that yelling comes from. We find that it comes from her deep desire to be the best mother ever. At a deep level, she told herself the story: "When my children misbehave, they are only doing this because I have messed up as a mother. Their naughty behaviour is proof that I am a bad mother." And so, out of this complex part she is not aware of, she needs to yell at them to tell herself it is her children's fault and not hers.

This mother yells at her children to prove she is not a bad mother.

Think about this. Yes, it didn't make much sense to the client either.

From there, we could further explore her insecurities of being a mother. Turns out that this had to do with her own experience of being parented by her mother, who was an alcoholic. Her mom parented multiple children on her own, without the resources required to be present and available. How does the next generation parent effectively when she has never had seen modelling of how to deal appropriately with the frustrations of misbehaving children?

Yes, we tracked the issues back to her mother—not to blame the mother, but to *target the healing.* By focusing in the appropriate place, this client can take responsibility for her behaviour. She began to explore the messages she is tells herself in ways that will create space for different behaviors.

Several months ago, I heard a lovely woman in her early 20s tell her story of struggle to a large gathering. She had a severe eating disorder and had reached the point where life didn't feel worth the struggle. Her self-described rock bottom moment found her in a hospital room after a desperate attempt to end the pain, with a profound and deep knowing that, "Nobody loves me. Nobody cares about me."

From there she began a slow road to recovery, where she realized her own value. Over time, she formed better and healthier relationships with herself, her family and a Power bigger than herself.

What made listening to this experience so fascinating to me is this: I knew of her parents. They are relatives of good friends of mine. Wonderful people. Caring people. I know that these parents are people that love their children and would move heaven and earth to help their children.

I have no doubt of these 3 things:
1. She felt utterly alone and unloved in her world—and those very painful feelings led her to despair and to do things that were desperate.
2. Her parents always deeply and profoundly loved her and would have been doing their best to make her know that.
3. There was a serious disconnect in how they felt about her and how she thought they felt about her.

As a counselor, I am listening for people's perceptions and experiences of how they have been hurt. I am aware that sometimes there has been actual and horrific abuse, real hurts, tangible neglect. I am also aware that children remember the significant events the best they can, but through the filters of a child. The vivid way these stories are encoded into their brain absolutely affected them. There is no way to know if it happened exactly like they remembered it.

A friend of a friend purchased the home I had lived in when I was a very young child! She invited me over to see it as an adult. I remember going into the house where I spent my preschool years. It shocked me how much smaller the rooms had become in the decades since I was a toddler! The rooms were laid out as I remembered them, but the stairs were narrower, the living room was undersized, and the kitchen was tiny. I remembered that home as a big old house in which there was ample room to run around. Was I wrong?

It's not important for a counselor to know if it happened exactly the way it was described because they are not judge or jury. A therapist's sole goal is to help a person grow and heal. If the client remembers something in a certain way that causes pain, that's what we have to work with. The pain is real—and so healing it is important. We are getting to the root cause of the pain which creates the problem. The pain matters because of how the person might have been affected by what they remember happened. The treatment focus is on healing the pain—not on the blame.

It would be unethical for a therapist to say, "Yes, this is all your mother's fault" and then send you away with the job done.

The therapist is far more likely to say, "Now that you appreciate where that behaviour/feeling/thought comes from, we have the ability to identify how to move forward. You no longer will be hijacked by it operating on your behalf. We will use this information to help you figure out how to move forward so that your thoughts, feelings, and actions are more in alignment with who you really are."

With conscious awareness becomes mindful responsibility.

The responsibility becomes yours. The responsibility is not your mother's (or father, or grandmother, or older brother, or schoolyard bully or whoever else has caused you pain) once you explore and understand what is happening in your life. Far from blaming your mother, therapy puts the responsibility for your life squarely in your lap.

And isn't taking responsibility what you really want?

10 It isn't my problem

Carter, my youngest son runs *hot*.

Ever since he was an infant, he has hates to overheat. Other babies were swaddled in receiving blankets under crocheted blankets, after they were dressed in undershirts and a sleeper.

My kid? He had on a diaper and a thin sleeper.

Other moms looked at me wondering if I cared about this child. After all—I dressed myself in about three layers holding a near naked baby. I run cold generally and am always looking for an extra sweater or a pair of warm slippers.

But I knew my boy—and he was comfortable when the rest of us were freezing. If I wanted a happy baby, I never put long sleeves on him. And the day I tried a turtleneck shirt was a day I immediately learned how **not** to dress my child! (Even though he was so darn cute in it!)

I loved the adorable overalls and he found them too hot. I loved some long-sleeved shirts which he automatically vetoed. (Doubly vetoed if they had a tag inside the neck.)

I didn't want the fights about clothing. As he grew older and became school aged, I established a rule: I decided he wore long pants to school when it was five degrees or more below freezing temperature. If it was less than five degrees below freezing, he could decide.

Practically, what it meant was that he wore shorts until the sidewalk puddles were solid.

Shorts made him happy, even when there was a thin layer of ice over the puddles, because he wasn't hot. The worst thing in life, at least for him to tell it, is for him to be too hot.

We have continued to deal with the implications of this as he has grown up. He's a competitive volleyball player, and I often picked him up from practice in high school.

I would be cold from being in and out of the car in winter. Often, I ran errands on my way to pick him up. I was in and out of the car repeatedly, letting all the cold air in. Cold feet in and out on cold concrete. Gloves had to come off as I'm loading and unloading, locking and unlocking. I never seemed to really warm up in the car before I was back out in the cold walking across icy parking lots. While I waited inside the gym for practice's end and for my son to change clothes, any heat in the car that had been created quickly dissipated in the evening's chill.

And then he and I would get into the car. Me, who is firmly chilly for some time. Cold hands, frozen feet. And Carter—who has just spent 2 hours jumping, running, going through assigned drills and generally being very physical. He's roasting. The underside of his hair is damp, his face is flushed, and he's warm—*really warm*—uncomfortably so, really. He **actually has steam** coming off him when we get in the car.

Picture the two of us in the same vehicle, inches away from the other. I'm driving, I've been in the vehicle, and I've already adjusted the air temperature on the drive over—fairly warm with a moderate rate of the fan. The heat has got the potential to get me comfortable, and maybe thaw my toes—with *time*.

We haven't got *time*. Carter feels the car's moderate heat amping up his own already steaming body. So—as we talk about the gym and the errands, saying nothing, he opens his window a few inches. The fresh, cold air washes over his glowing brow, beginning to cool him.

This cold air blasts not just the over-heated him, but also the under-heated me.

It gets colder—we're still talking about the latest antics of the athletes during the drills and enjoying the day. My hand naturally, without conscious thought, closes in on the dial to notch up the heat to further warm the air.

What happens? You guessed it—his window opens further—just a few more inches. And I turn up the level of the fan.

We are still having a friendly banter about our lives, but within minutes, with no discussion on the topic, there has been a *silent, elaborate temperature dance.*

The result is that the car is blasting hot air at gale force while simultaneously being wind whipped with frigid air through the passenger side window which is now wide open.

Sort of hilarious once we noticed—but not comfortable for either of us.

Each one was compensating for the adjustments of the other, with the internal weather conditions getting gradually more and more extreme—and while each of us was adjusting to improve conditions. Let's just say, well— our efforts were individually and collectively unsuccessful.

We were both working to fix the situation—but were locked into a pattern that was actually making it worse for both of us.

Counterbalancing another's actions by equal and opposite reactions is a solution of sorts. However, it is an awkward and difficult-to-sustain strategy. Rather like two people standing precariously in a canoe. One leans one way, the other leans in the opposite direction and the other responds— until both are barely hanging on. The canoe stays balanced—but at a huge price:

- Parents—when A is so lenient to the child, B feels the need to be stricter, and so A becomes more lenient to compensate. B reacts with further rigidity—and so on, and so on.

- Partners—A feels the other is passive and so yells at other with a bit of an edge to "poke" B to respond. B can sense the escalation, and doesn't like where this is going, so takes a deep breath, and further retreats to avoid a blowout. Spouse A notices the withdrawal and so feels even more responsible for making something happen, and so goes after B with a stronger reaction. Spouse B senses further escalation and so—well, you know the drill by now.

- At work—A notices B is very laid back. A develops lists and hard timelines and schedules meetings to help the team get on top of things. Employee B is annoyed by how "Type A" that Worker A is and blows off all the lists and timelines and meetings. This further demonstrates to A just how very irresponsible B is, and so A puts more details into the lists, and the timelines get more rigid.

In the middle of this silent crazy dance Carter and I were having, we suddenly looked at each other and laughed.

I made the first move—and told him I'd turn the heat down, if he would roll up the window.

I knew it would not be as warm as I wanted it, and I think Carter knew it would not be as cold as he wanted it. But we both knew that if we tolerated something somewhere in the middle, we'd both enjoy the ride a lot more than these swirling waves of hot and freezing gales that had been blowing simultaneously around the vehicle. It may not have been my perfect temperature, but I had a satisfaction in knowing that some of my discomfort contributed to his ability to tolerate the ride better.

So—whose fault is the lousy temperature in the car? And really, who gets to decide what temperature is the wrong one in this car? Believe me, I had days of picking Carter up, when I knew that this ungrateful kid should put up with the heat because he should be grateful he had a mom that was willing to pick him up! (Yes, I am not always empathic and understanding when I am cold. I become a lean, mean, blaming machine, like anybody else!)

And if you asked him, I was being completely unreasonable to heat the car to volcanic levels, especially considering "Prickly Heat Syndrome", a diagnosis he and a friend gave themselves. They throw this term around like it is a prized obscure potentially-fatal diagnosis from Mayo Clinic that I need to respect and treat.

So often problems lie within the relationship dynamic.

The problem exists in the patterns *between* the people more often than *inside* of the people themselves.

For example, a husband wants sex more often and hints at the same to his wife. The next day, he goes to embrace her warmly, she pulls away. She wants intercourse less often—the kids, the job, the house—she's exhausted. She avoids the hug to avoid giving him something that could slide into a sexual encounter. It's intended as a kindness—she will sacrifice being hugged so as not to lead him on unfairly. She loves the hugs but wants it to be merely a hug that night, not foreplay, so she spurns all contact. But he feels the distance and feels rejected. That hurts, especially when it happens again.

Now he is angry that she is avoiding him and confronts her to tell her he needs sex more often. (He wants to be close to her but he can't tell her softly and openly how much he misses this closeness because that's too hard when he's so hurt. It's difficult to feel lonely and feel so vulnerable that you can't admit it.)

You can imagine, with little difficulty, her response to his demand to be close. She feels pressured to have sex. She further pulls away and now can't even imagine wanting a hug. Now she doesn't sit on the same couch as he does in the evening. She goes to bed before him to avoid intimacy.

Eventually they don't even end their day with the casual conversation that used to draw them together.

A couple's therapist will help you understand the patterns you are locked into that create withdrawal and pursuit that results in discomfort for you both.

- A wife who feels ignored and neglected as her husband works too many hours complains to him about how he isn't an attentive husband. He doesn't know what she wants, and so it's easier for him to stay late and work on the project. His boss is excited about and pleased with how it's going and regularly affirms his work ethic and good progress, and that feels great.

- A husband feels like his wife is micro-managing his life in a way that feels restrictive and mistrustful. He is resentful and begins to hide his phone so she can't see it. And sometimes will come home an hour later without telling her why because he wants a bit of his own space. She increases the intensity of her supervisory activities which further increases his desperate desire to not have her know everything. Therapy will reveal that years ago he had some inappropriate kisses with a female colleague. We will also discover the wife has recently come to know a new female has begun in his department. She is fearful—and she remembers now that she watched her mother over-function when her parents were fighting as a solution. It was her mother's way to cope

- A wife is drinking more and more, at first on weekends, and then even during the week. The husband feels the effects of her paying more attention to alcohol than the relationship, and he starts to cajole her to drink less. He buys her flowers and makes dinner when she doesn't—he doesn't complain because he watched his father leave his mother after many loud arguments. The husband dilutes the alcohol and often pours her the drinks so he can ensure there isn't much in the glass. He tries harder and harder to be the husband that she might need him to be to stop drinking. Her consumption continues to increase.

Do you see how the problem is the *pattern*—the way spouses connect with each other? A couples' therapist looks at the dynamics of what is happening in the couple relationship.

Couples come to me with issues about budgeting, or sex, or even who takes out the garbage. Almost always we can see that the connection between the two people is damaged by the patterns they are locked into.

As we understand the pattern, then remove/heal the underlying reasons that create the pattern, new patterns emerge, the connection is regained—and the couple returns to therapy having addressed who takes out the garbage without any help.

Please note: This is **not** about blaming the victim. (Classic example: "I wouldn't have hit you if you hadn't burnt the roast"). Abuse doesn't rise as a natural response to the pattern—it's **not** "your fault" when your partner abuses you. However, even in abusive situations, without realizing it, we teach people how to treat us. (Relationships earlier in our lives often teach us how we should be treated.)

We all take part in creating dynamics in the relationship, which gives permission for uncomfortable or painful situations to occur. It is not your responsibility to get him/her to stop abusing you. However, a therapist wants to work with you to help you find your own ability to effect change. A therapist explores how much you believe in yourself. A therapist explores how the relationship has affected you, making it harder for you to remove yourself from an unhealthy relationship.

Sometimes it is possible to establish a healthier relationship. Sometimes, changing the dynamics so you aren't being hurt/abused means the relationship will not continue.

A family therapist will explore the dynamic between parent and child, or sister and brother. You and the therapist will seek to understand the patterns and tensions, the ways in which actions are working to achieve a purpose other than what's immediately apparent.

The family therapist sees a family rather like a small mobile of critters that hangs from the ceiling over a bassinet. When the bear gets yanked over here, the rabbit swings over there, and the pig jiggles over there.

The family therapist sees this one mobile of critters as one arm hanging from a larger mobile that is comprised of several mobiles…classroom, grandparents, soccer team, workplace. That mobile is, in turn, hanging from another arm of an even larger mobile: school, extended family, community club. And that mobile is an arm of a still larger mobile—cultural norms and political climate.

- A child acts out at school with bullying and cheating on tests. The parents bring the child in, and as we work with the family, we come to understand that the child notices that when the school calls home, the parents work together to solve the problems with the child at school. This collaboration is a welcome relief for the child who is terrified by his parent's constant fights. The child's behaviour at school improves as the therapist helps the parents resolve their issues.

A newly married couple, each with their own biological school-aged children who live in the home with them, come to therapy because his children are acting out at home. He works extensive hours, leaving her to parent his children with very little relationship having developed. When he is home, he is tired, and she still does the bulk of the parenting. He hangs back from parenting. His children don't feel as connected to him and resent her. This all happens in a world when men do the travelling and women do the parenting—even when it makes more sense for the father to take the lead parenting his own biological children in a new step-family situation.

The long and short of it is this: It simply makes little sense to say, "There is no point in going to counseling because it is someone else's fault". Their behaviour may be a huge problem for you and others. However, as someone who is swinging from the same mobile, you can benefit from exploring your actions and reactions.

- Wouldn't it be helpful for you to know how your actions affect the system, and where your actions and reactions come from?
- Wouldn't you want to look at your role in the pattern that has developed?
- Wouldn't you want to understand better how doing your own work might impact on a painful situation involving someone else in your life?

A good therapist won't turn around and blame you. A therapist will help work with you to understand how you may perpetuate painful patterns in painful relationships that aren't working for you.

A couples therapist or a family therapist may work with the system—the dyad of the two of you—or with your family to do that work together with all of you.

Therapy isn't a court of law. It's a place of healing.

In the end, in counseling, it's generally irrelevant whose fault it is. What is important is getting yourself (and perhaps others too) in a better place in your life.

11 I should be able to fix this myself

If you have children, do you remember that stage when every other word that came out of their mouths was, "Me! I do it myself!"? They want to tie their shoelaces on their own, cut their meat, go up the stairs without the handrail or your hand. It is a painstakingly difficult phase when, as a parent, you either endure the toddler's attempt to do it on his/her own, or bring on the meltdown by doing it for them—or both. When a child struggles to tie their laces when their fingers just can't move as precisely as their brains tell them, they fail.

We understand the toddler's desire to have independence. We love learning to do something on our own. We love mastery, that hard-won victorious sense of having developed proficiency after struggling to learn something. That feeling of, "Myself!" doesn't go away when you become an adult.

I recently learned Sudoku, a number puzzle with 9 squares of 9 squares, each needing the digits of 1-9 arranged in the square. No digit is repeated in a row up and down, left to right, or within the square of 9. I've observed my dad playing Sudoku for years, and I was never interested. Not long ago, on vacation, I was sitting in an airplane puzzling over this Sudoku thing in my son Jay's book as I was passing the time enroute to our family vacation destination. My adolescent son laughed at my ineptness, took the book from me, and in a flash, had over half the puzzle done, explaining as he went. I stared with fascination how he had strategies and techniques to do this puzzle while I stared blankly at the page.

I hate it when someone can do something well that I can't do at all, when I know I have the capability to learn. Jay knew something I didn't.

Game on!!

I've spent the last 6 weeks doing Sudoku puzzles here and there. I've moved to progressively harder puzzles to further develop my abilities to solve these problems.

I understand that my Sudoku solving skills are relatively useless in the rest of the world. This is a skill that serves little point other than to prove to myself that I have developed it.

But I take some pride in the satisfaction of being able to struggle my way through a puzzle with some knowledge and expertise. It is a far cry from my blank stare less than two months ago.

Don't we all love to solve problems, and to solve them independently, on our own? Most of us love the pleasure of having attacked the problem, generated strategies, and then implemented a solution. When something finally works for me, there is a little party in my brain.

Somehow, somewhere, though, we have acquired the idea that a problem is best solved on our own. That the victory of accomplishment means more if we solve problems on our own. That the satisfaction is sweeter if we did it without help.

How did we get there?

❧❧

I watched a story on the news a couple of years ago and discovered Allison, the turtle. I dug a little deeper and viewed a YouTube video about Allison and her impediment[ii]. Allison only had one flipper. A shark attack had left her with three stumps.

When a turtle has one flipper, there is only one option, really. Picture it—a turtle flapping one flipper, again and again.

Circles, circles, and more circles.

The guy, Jeff George, at the turtle refuge at South Padre Island was clear:

- turtles with three flippers can get released back in the wild,
- turtle with two flippers can probably make it in the turtle sanctuary

But,

- turtles with one flipper—not much hope.

Turtles with one flipper are generally euthanized.

They tried prostheses with Allison—but there wasn't enough residual stump for them to work. She is a one flipper turtle. No options.

One of the young interns remembered something though. An intern—just a kid, really—you know, the sort of person who no one might think to listen to.

The intern recalled his days as a kid—rowing with one paddle in an inner tube. Think about it, use your imagination. A kid, rowing with the paddle in an inner tube over and over equals circles, only circles.

Just like a one-flippered turtle. But put a kid in a canoe, and rowing with a single paddle is doable. The difference lies in the canoe's length. The vehicle acts as a rudder, giving direction to the momentum created by the paddle.

This intern thought outside the box, with a fresh perspective from those who just have always used prosthesis with turtles missing limbs. The intern worked with a wet suit that had a rudder. The staff played with the positioning and size, and one day-VOILA!!

Allison has become a coordinated turtle. She can go where she wants in the tank. She feeds herself. Allison decides when to dive and when to surface, and then does it, on her own.

She still only has one flipper.

But—it took someone with a fresh perspective to help Allison with some different possibilities. The interview I heard talked about how the handlers continue to marvel at how Allison has "perked up", how she revels in her mobility. She is a new turtle with her rudder. The single fin isn't so much a problem anymore.

This story reminded me of some moments I have had with clients, when a comment or question I ask helps them understand the issue through fresh ideas.

Therapists aren't so brilliant as to identify exactly what everybody should do all the time. They study their craft and strive towards excellence, but they can't tell the future, read your mind, or know what should be done in every situation.

Nobody goes to therapy to hear someone who has all the answers.

That's disrespectful to clients who spend all day every day living their lives, having the challenging relationships, or experiencing the depression, or struggling not to give in to drinking the alcohol threatening to destroy their lives. I believe that clients have a wisdom about their own lives. They live every moment of every day with the problems and issues that bring them to therapy. If a simple response was that obvious, would they even need to come to therapy?

If it was as simple as someone saying, "Don't do A, choose B, and then your life will be a much easier", wouldn't everybody know to just choose B? Of course!

Clients are looking for support, not easy answers.

Easy answers, when they exist (and sometimes they do!) are acted upon immediately by people without ever becoming clients. You don't need therapy for that.

But we can all get stuck in thinking about complicated situations in a rigid way. A therapist concentrates carefully, asking questions and hearing things from a different perspective. It can open up dialogue and fresh options in a way that still trusts the client to solve the problems.

The fresh perspective the client gains leaves them in a better position to move forward in positive directions in their lives.

When that happens, clients practically bound out of a session with fresh energy, ready to tackle life. It's fun to watch—kind of like it is fun to watch Allison.

Several years ago, I was presented with a project. It was a huge venture that was intimidating in scope, but also had huge opportunities. The possibilities were enormous and the outcome had a chance of being awesome. However, it would take me in new directions, and ask a lot of me.

There were legitimate concerns about the logistics. All in all, it was a risky project—that someone was working hard to talk me into.

I spent weeks going back and forth on how to proceed. Should I, or shouldn't I? I was wrestling with joining the project, with my question to myself, over and over, "Can I do it?" and, "Could I pull it off?"

I grappled with its do-ability. I contemplated whether I could do it. And I wasn't sure. I was hesitant.

Then a colleague, chatting with me one afternoon, asked me: "What if you asked, 'Do I *want* to do this project?' rather than, '*Can* I do this project?'

The lights flashed on!

The instant I asked myself the question, "Do I want to do this project?", everything shifted. I knew I didn't want to do it. Despite the cajoling and convincing of others, my heart wasn't in it. I didn't believe enough in the project, didn't think it was a good use of my time, and the outcomes were far more important to others than myself.

It took someone outside of the situation, someone with greater distance from the project than me, to notice that there was another way of approaching the decision. Another person had a wisdom I could not have had, to ask a different question. I was too close and too involved, to recognize an alternate approach. She gave me an invaluable perspective that changed the course.

Once I knew I didn't want to do the project, regardless of if I could do it, it was obvious I would decline the opportunity.

The one question by a colleague changed an agonizing decision into a simple one.

How is a person supposed to know what they know and don't know? How can anyone know what they don't know? And yet why do we expect ourselves to know what we don't know? Everyone has blind spots. Spots that we can't see for ourselves.

By definition, we can't see our own blind spots. How could we?

Inviting someone into an area of your life where you seldom, if ever, let someone in, can allow someone to notice the blind spots.

A therapist will often interrupt a client in the telling of their story. You know how people have a certain, specific script? It might be the story of how her husband left her or the story of how the cancer got diagnosed and treatment began. They've told the story a dozen times. Maybe a hundred times. As the story is recounted repeatedly, the story takes on a personality of its own. It is told in a certain way—which gives us fixed way of seeing the characters in the story, and the outcome of the story.

In counseling, the therapist will ask questions or notice parts of the story that are often neglected, or under-told, or even missed altogether. The fresh questions change the way a person tells the story to him/herself.

I had a client who came to therapy after not having attended for a couple of years. He had been to see me a few times and then said he had to stop coming because life was too overwhelming. Life had dealt him a bad hand. His wife had a long serious illness. This client's business was struggling to survive. He had also taken on a major debt of a summer house that now hung like a noose around his neck. His world collapsed when his business had a fire and water damage destroyed all his business documents. He was dealing with insurance and trying to manage a business that barely surviving with no documentation. He was swamped and had put therapy on the back burner. And now, after the chaos and its demands on his time had subsided, he returned.

He told me that the last session we had before he didn't return for 2 years had been profound for him. This client shared his vivid recollection of a conversation from our last meeting all those many months ago. He said that as he was telling me his story of one bad and exhausting thing happening after another, I had asked him: "Wow, how is it you can even get out of bed every morning?!"

He recounted how, in that moment, he couldn't recall how he answered the question, but the question stuck with him. And he realized that as unanswerable the question was, given the situation, I could only ask it because, in fact, he had gotten out of bed that morning. The question was one of compassion for how tough his life was, and one of admiration and curiosity about how he prevailed against such difficulty. This gentleman told me that that question stayed with him every day as an encouragement of sorts. It reminded him that, as difficult as it was, he had made it through another day.

Knowing that question could even be asked of him during such a difficult time gave him hope that sustained him during a very difficult season of his life.

❧ ❧

I work a lot with couples, and couples often find the support of a therapist valuable in having them see new perspectives.

Picture this: A newlywed couple comes to see me because he is not initiating sex with her. She wonders if she is unattractive, if she is somehow pushing him away without realizing it. She longs to be close and intimate with her husband in every way. She is confused why she is being rejected. Part of couple therapy explores his feelings towards her. He loves her deeply. She is unlike any woman he has ever been with—kinder and gentler. He admires her goodness and her loveliness. He sees her as so pure and wonderful and has her on such a pedestal he doesn't feel he can approach her. Through our conversation, he is able to tell her (and himself) that he doesn't feel worthy of intimacy with her because she is so remarkable. She is dumbfounded that he would perceive her that way. Therapy progresses once we are able to determine this.

A fresh telling of the story, with fresh questions to change the way you tell your story and hear your story as you tell it, creates fresh discoveries.

Everyone needs some help once in a while to solve a tough situation in new ways. Ask around. It's smart to ask for help to see into your blind spots.

Try asking for a fresh idea.

12 Therapy is expensive

I'm biased and I know it.

I'll be transparent about my opinion of the cost of therapy at the outset:

I think the value of therapy is a little like those credit card commercials where they show how much the beach mat cost, how much gas cost to get to the beach, the hotel rate, how much the umbrella and sand toys cost, announce the price of the overpriced hot dog and lemonade and then they show the unbridled joy in the toothy grin of a preschooler whose body has sand in every conceivable crevice. All this is wrapped up with the caption: "Priceless".

You can't put a price on therapy when it changes your life course, gives you peace of mind that you haven't had before, or decreases the tension in an important relationship. The value of therapy is priceless.

Some of you will be fortunate to have low cost or free counseling services available to you, perhaps through your Employee and Family Assistance Plan (EFAP) at work, or through the school counseling services or the local clinic. Some of you have the patience of the biblical figure of Job and will wait a ridiculously long time in the queue until your name comes up at the local free clinic.

There will be others who have the financial abilities to invest in good therapy as chump change. When you don't have to budget the cost of therapy into your life, that is indeed, a privilege!

But for everybody else, therapy is pricey! The rest of us, should we choose to invest in it, do some serious budget development as part of figuring out how to make it work. And sometimes, for many of us, the cost of therapy is exorbitant. And it *may be simply too much.*

Years ago, when my children were in elementary school, my husband at the time went through a fall on the ice, had a difficult winter, and at the end of it, decided he needed to make his own home away from me.

I felt like I had been hit by a bus. I craved a six-month coma as I sought to avoid the intensity of the pain and terror I felt every second of every day. I was facing life without the man with whom I fully intended to grow old. The distress took a toll on my body: I lost 30 pounds; I woke up with a pit in my stomach at about 4 in the morning most days and couldn't fall back to sleep.

My life frightened me.

I was single parenting children who were experiencing their own real turmoil. I was in over my head. I needed some perspective that a therapist could give me.

I was working in private practice as a therapist at the time. Trust me—I did my best to pull myself together during the day to give my clients my very best therapeutic work. Every day I worked with people who paid me good money and invested time to do quality therapy. I took that seriously and was deliberate in putting my troubles off to the side to enter the world of my client for the hour. I like to think I became more compassionate towards the pain of my clients.

And every day I thought to myself: "I desperately need a therapist of my own right now. But—*I can't afford* **me.**" I had expenses for a house purchased with two incomes in mind, children who had music lessons and growing feet, and now lawyer bills. That was a stark reality for me when I knew I couldn't pay for the counseling services I needed and that I provided to others.

I got resourceful and looked at alternatives. It was an undeserved grace to be allowed to work with an excellent therapist that had public funding. I could only go about every 6 weeks, given the heavy demands of his schedule. But the therapy I received that season from him over about a half dozen sessions provided some real grounding and support. My fantastically loyal friends couldn't and wouldn't have had those conversations with me.

Sometimes, you need people to express the hard things to you—which supportive friends may shy away from. My therapist challenged the way I saw things in ways I never would have heard the same way from my friends. It was wonderful to have had several sessions with him. Priceless, really. There were a few comments he made that helpfully echoed in my head for years.

I am grateful. And my gratitude has shaped my practice. I provide a lower cost option at my private practice. (We engage an intern for that work.) Personally, I provide a limited number of spaces myself for reduced rate therapy as part of *paying it forward*. I think it's important for a therapist to make therapy possible for people who lose their jobs or suddenly find themselves looking after a full family on half the income when a spouse leaves.

Most of us have to make sacrifices to make therapy fit in the budget. Fewer meals out. A cheaper vacation. Maybe even no vacation. We need to plan and budget because good quality therapy isn't cheap. There may be times and places where the therapy is funded, but *someone* is always paying hefty amounts for therapy.

Therapists go to school for many years to develop and hone their craft. After graduation, there is ongoing professional development. Therapists spend many hours of clinical supervision with a more experienced therapist to further develop their expertise and uncover blind spots as they are working. Therapists are expected, ethically and often legally, to be a lifelong learners. This means that therapists sign up for professional development courses online, locally, or sometimes across the country. This keeps your therapist fresh and invigorated, up to date with the latest evidence in the research and current with the latest developments in clinical models. Therapists work to be at the top of their game to better serve the client.

In short, therapy is expensive because therapists receive training at great expense—and they have mortgages, grocery bills and utilities like anybody else. Add to that, the therapy almost always happens in a room that requires heating/cooling, lights, rent, and administrative support. *There are few therapists that are dripping in diamonds and I don't know any with yachts or private islands.* The therapists I know have worked hard, often at great sacrifice to do the meaningful work that they get to do.

(As an aside, there are lots of professions that may be more financially lucrative. However, I am honoured to have a front-row seat in the lives of folks who yearn to connect more meaningfully with themselves and others. I have a career I wouldn't trade for anything!)

જીજી

With the substantial cost of therapy, often folks work to get by without it. They talk to friends, read books, surf the internet for good resources. These can be excellent and be the assistance some individuals require.

However, when:

- your marriage is falling apart
- your son barely acknowledges you exist
- your depression is so crippling you may soon not be able to get out of bed at all
- your anxiety is so high you now have anxiety about how much this is stressing your body
- you are new in town and don't have deep friendships to share hard stuff with
- relationships of depth are something you want, but don't know where to start, and you're lonely and there is no one you can talk to about it.

Self-help resources may not be enough, and it makes sense to figure out a way to get yourself on a therapist's couch. We were meant to work through our internal stuff in connection with another. We do better in community.

You might be doing the best you can, and it may even be working to some extent. The relationship is struggling, but often folks are creative, and do some work-arounds:

- Your wife really isn't happy with you, and is threatening divorce, but you take on extra projects at work. By working more, you increase your income which makes her happier. Your being out of the house decreases the tension that exists when the two of you spend too much time together

- The relationship with your son is lousy and the only time the two of you seem to talk is when he feels that you are criticizing him for something. So, you stop harping on him, and let him play video games until all hours of the night and sleep all day. He rarely leaves the house.

- The depression feels terrible, but if you stay busy and productive enough at work, it pushes those feelings of feelings of self-hatred away. The boss likes your work and the odd tidbit of praise can keep you from drowning in the sea of hopeless and helplessness—as long as you find a way to stave off complete exhaustion.

- The anxiety feels oppressive and full-on anxiety attacks often seem at the edge of possibility. However, when you smoke weed, the edge of it gets taken off and life is liveable again. There is no risk of anxiety attacks when high on pot, which is nearly all the time now. There's not much chance of getting employment either.

Sometimes *something* works but isn't a *sustainable or realistic* solution.

I was at a parking lot in a shopping center a few years ago, when a Good Samaritan passing by let me know that the passenger side rear tire was low. I don't go around that side of the car really and so I really appreciated his noticing and telling me.

He was being polite. It wasn't just *low.*

I think it was close to *flat.* I drove slowly and carefully to the gas station close by, and they filled it up for me. They checked to make sure it had the right pressure. The gas jockey let me know I should check it frequently over the next while in case it had a slow leak. The other tires had normal pressure when we made sure they were OK. (Well, not *we*, it was actually *him*.)

I checked that freshly pumped tire several times over the next few days and it looked OK—for a while.

About 5 days later, the pressure had dropped to about a 1/3 of what it should be. I went to another gas station and filled it up again. I knew what to do this time.

The next day, the air pressure was visibly lower. So, I searched for a gas station filled the tire up with air.

The car was good to drive. It was perfectly safe to drive, except this *filling up the tire with air* was getting to be a bit of a pain.

It started to need me to pump air every day and a half or so.

As I was going about my day, I was driving slowly by gas stations to check to see if they had an air machine. My thoughts while driving, even while listening to the news, or singing tunes, or chatting with the person beside me, frequently went to that passenger side tire.

That tire preoccupied my thoughts. I was wondering about the tire pressure whenever I was in the vehicle: "Was it low? When had I last checked? Was I being overly pessimistic and concerned? Was I being overly optimistic and had overlooked the sponginess of the tire?" I started circling the car every time I got in. The car was safe to drive, and I was keeping it safe to drive, but *this was no way to live.*

The tire was where it should be—it was full and operational—but the strategy I was using was costly. It increased my vigilance and created hassle as I searched for the tire gauge and found a pump.

It *worked*, even though *it wasn't really working.*

I took it in to a tire shop, and the mechanics there had it fixed in a couple of hours. They found a nail. They patched it. Done. $22.

I could have just kept filling the tire with air when it needed it. That was free.

It would've been cheaper. But it would have been more expensive to my mental and physical health to keep filling it with air. This occurred in the middle of a Canadian winter! Who wants to be filling tires in snowy weather?!

By now, you understand that this story isn't about tires.

I work with couples who have been filling the air in the tires of their marriage desperately—trying to make it move forward safely, but at great personal cost. It's difficult to address a marital flat tire with Band-Aids, though I've heard stories of people trying. They put in a ton of effort for not-a-lot of results.

- A husband hears his disgruntled wife grumble about him, and so starts spending more time with the guys. He stays home one night a week with the kids so she can go out with her girlfriends. It sort of works. She's happy when she gets out with her friends, and he really enjoys the stress-free time with the guys. But the disgruntlement between the two of them always returns.
- A wife sees her husband pulling away and is distant. She buys a new negligee, gets a babysitter, and gives him a night he won't soon forget. He likes it but it doesn't last. Two days later he has pulled away as far as he has ever been.

I've worked with individuals too, who solve slow leaks in the tires of the lives in ways other than finding the leak. They bump along with a strategy that makes it better for a bit by

- going shopping—all of life's troubles disappear when you rock a new pair of pumps
- going on-line to view endless amount of porn, fantasizing about intimacy with another while completely pulling away from real connection in the real world,
- drinking too much
- using perfectionism to drive away that "not enough" feeling

Ultimately any of these leaves a person feeling lonely and empty and back where they started. The tire of life is still leaking fast—or flat.

What do you do to deal with the pain, anxiety, depression, loss, fear, trauma, or broken relationships in your life?

What strategies do you use to get through the day?

How much do your strategies actually cost you financially? Psychologically? Relationally? Emotionally? Spiritually? Physically?

Is it worth it? Can you afford *not* to go to therapy?

The patch cost $22—the air was free.

It cost me an afternoon—instead of 5-7 minutes at a time (multiple times).

To be clear, in the long run, when I measure my quality of life, the patch was immeasurably cheaper.

A therapist might truly be priceless. Especially because that way you'll be able to stop spinning your tires.

(Sorry, pun was intended!)

13 I might cry

There is something about our culture that has people feel that crying in front of others should not happen. Typically, when someone feels the urge to cry when someone else is around, they seek to stifle the feeling. A person feels the lump at the back of their throat, or senses tears at the back of their eyes and the automatic feeling is to push it down. Maybe that person distracts themselves by changing the topic either in their head or out loud, or by forcing themselves to switch from that which triggers tears to something that is lighter or more neutral.

Then, if that the person is unsuccessful, if a person's eyes fill with tears that threaten to spill over despite their best efforts, what happens next?

Yes, you guessed it—the apology. Almost immediately people express an apology for crying.

A person, starting to cry in the presence of others, almost always says: "I'm sorry", as if they have made a mistake with crying. It is as though the tears are offensive and hurtful to the other. As if crying is wrong.

Many people avoid crying even when they are by themselves. Even when there is no one to watch, they stand in judgement of themselves. Somehow, many view crying as a flaw, or a weakness and something to avoid. Crying is somehow seen as frightening. It is as though the act of crying will somehow create cracks in a person's wellbeing and create mental instability.

If the world sees crying as so dysfunctional, I can understand why people wouldn't want to go to therapy.

Fear of tears is one reason people avoid counseling. A person often has an inherent awareness that once they allow themselves to go to internal places long ignored, the tears will materialize. Clients let themselves acknowledge the pain of hurts long ago—of schoolyard bullying, the judgement of a parent, or moving away from childhood security. When, at last, a person give voice to the sadness that is otherwise pushed down every other minute of every other day, tears are freed to emerge. Somehow saying it out loud heightens their impact. When you talk about what's inside, it's as though you give it permission to be. When you name an emotion, it is a gift to the part of you feeling that emotion. The act of naming a feeling often gives that emotion permission to be more felt.

It is not uncommon, even in the first 5 minutes of the first therapy session, as I acknowledge and honor the courage of the client sitting across to me, that chins wobble. As I let people know that doing the difficult work of showing up to name and process something in their life that isn't working is admirable and courageous, their eyes get red. If the light is just right, I can see the extra glistening in their eyes of tears collecting at their bottom lid.

Immediately, I can see the steely-faced efforts to make the face to stop the chin wobble and put the tear ducts on ice. People look up to stop the tears from escaping their eye balls. They look away to decrease the intensity of the moment, to allow themselves to regain their composure.

Yes, that's it. Composure. What's so scary about crying in therapy is that a person might lose their composure. Even the term, *losing your composure* sounds vulnerable. No one likes to lose anything in front of anybody. How much do people hate losing their ability to look like they have it all together?

Enough to make sure they don't cry in front of others—including a therapist. For some, that's sufficient reason to say, "Nope" to therapy.

Don't we all hate when other people can see us struggling? Is there a bigger indicator to struggle than tears? It feels so vulnerable when other people can see our softest, most tender spots. Crying leaves a person feeling so exposed.

So, when you say you won't go to counseling, you might tell yourself that you can't go to counseling because you have bowling, or take up bowling (or lawn darts or square dancing or, well—something!!) or that it will cut into your reading time. (With a note to self that you'd better start reading to make that excuse stick!)

When you say you won't go to counseling, maybe underneath that is the fear that *you will cry*. And when you are weeping, you will do so in front of a therapist who hardly knows you. And when that therapist sees you crying, you wonder what he or she will be thinking.

If you're like the rest of us, your automatic assumption will be that the therapist thinks you are a mess. You know that the therapist is seeing you as some whack-a-doodle. You will tell yourself the story that while the therapist is looking compassionate on the outside, internally they are shaking their head at the pathetic picture in front of them.

I know. Because I have been a client, and that's what I thought what my therapist would think if I started to weep. Most of the people who sit in my office and cry for the first time, without thinking, apologize to me and do their best to suppress their tears.

Please allow me to fill you in on how I see tears in the therapy office.

Tears of significance.

First, I know that when tears are present, it's only because those tears have been able to overcome the resistance of the person who is frantically resisting them. Those tears have persisted through the urges to push them down and not allow them to appear. Those tears are persistent and I know they are important. These tears have likely been waiting to spill over for eons.

When I see tears I know something important is happening. Tears tell that the client and I are exploring an area that matters. I know that the work we are doing impacts the person at a deep level when I hear a person's voice choke up and become tight.

While the tendency of the person who is crying is to apologize and change the topic to stop the tears, my tendency is to slow things down and *spend time where the tears are*. I do not intend to *make the person cry* or hurt them by spending time in hurting places. My intent is to release the tears and explore what the tears are trying to say.

Tears are a sign that we are on important ground. Tears indicate a sacred space that merits gentle and slow treading.

If the tears haven't been allowed to fall, then they haven't been allowed to speak either.

That probably sounds hokey to you, this therapist mumbo-jumbo is one reason you've been avoiding the likes of us. Can you give me a chance to explain?

Picture yourself like a house, made up of rooms. Some rooms have big windows and wide entrances letting you into the room. There are no doors at all.

Other rooms have a single small door, and it's padlocked. To open that room would involve tears falling. To avoid the tears, you avoid the room. You don't have full access to your house because you dare not unlock that door. It's brutal to go into a space that is unlocked only by tears. No one likes to do that. That's why it's better to open that door together with someone you trust. Someone who unlocks doors often and goes into that room for the first time with you.

Once the door is unlocked and tears are shed, the door to the room gets opened, and maybe even gets taken off. The room is now possible to enter, if you wish. If the room is about the death of a parent, it might be a chance to remember some special moments in the room, when you can look around in there. It creates an opportunity to remember important and helpful conversations, fun memories of vacations and beautiful moments with a loved parent, not just the painful final days of an illness.

The space may not be a place in which you want to hang out if the room was padlocked because of the pain of the trauma held within—like a sexual assault, or the substance abuse of a parent. But it actually feels safer and cozier to live in a house where the doors aren't locked tight and where you choose to have the door half closed. You may not hang out in that room by choice, but it doesn't have to be sealed to hold the fear and grief either.

Can you imagine the freedom?

Tears of relief

Did you ever get lost when you were a kid? Maybe for a few moments in an amusement park you started following the wrong pair of legs and when you looked up, it wasn't your mom? Or you stopped to look in a store window for a minute in a mall, but your dad didn't realize you weren't following him, and he disappeared into the sea of people?

Do you remember when you started to cry?

For most kids tears erupt at the moment they are found. When their mother crouches down and scoops them up and holds them in a tight embrace—that's when the waterworks start.

Before that, there is only terror. There is no room for sadness, only fear. It's all business until a child finds momma or poppa, and then they collapse into sobs. The safety of a parent's arms allows for the vulnerable feeling of sadness to emerge.

Safety is the key criteria for tears to fall. Sinking into soft feelings becomes possible, even probable, with safety.

It is not uncommon, in the safe cocoon of the therapy office, for a person to begin telling their story and find their eyes starting to leak profusely. They explain to me they told themselves they would not cry in the session and now reluctantly accept a tissue. It's as though the tears that have been held in a quiet, silent reservoir unnoticed, sometimes for decades, finally emerge in the safety of therapy. While it is uncomfortable to cry, there is a feeling of unburdening that happens. As the reservoir drains there is a calming release.

For many years I taught basic counseling skills to students at university. Every year the students would bring up the same concern: "What happens if I *make* a patient cry?" When they ask this question, it has an implied tone of horror about it. I think the students wondered if it was mean—or perhaps were already convinced it was cruelty. Every year, we would explore this question: "What happens if a patient/client cries while a therapist is with them?"

No doubt, there are terrible therapists who might *make* their clients cry with criticism and shaming. That's *not* cool—it's wrong. If that happens to you, on behalf of my profession, I'm sorry. I think this is actually rare.

So, I would process with the students by asking them, "If your client is telling a story, and you encourage further exploration, and a client's tears arise, what is happening?" The students always get to the realization that, most often, when a client cries, it is a sign that they feel safe enough to let the sadness or turmoil or depression or whatever voice to express itself. The tears, along with the grief or hurt were there, all along, just suppressed. Now those tears have the courage to emerge. Crying expresses something meaningful at the moment. They acknowledge feelings that have been held but unexpressed, all along.

At my office, we have facial tissues everywhere. Three boxes of tissues in each counseling room—one within easy reach of where the client sits. One is near the therapist to allow us to hand the box over to the client as needed. Sometimes, I need one myself in session since I'm human too. A third is on standby on the bottom shelf, waiting its turn. We have tissues in the waiting area and by the reception, too.

Around our office, tears are

- signs of vulnerability which we see as courage
- valued forms of expression
- signs of trust in the therapist and in the therapy—and therefore are valued
- evidence that a person's soul is daring to express itself. It is a sign of poignancy
- little symbols of something important—and so each tear holds an exquisite dignity

Clients tell me they fear that if they start to cry, they might never stop. The tears have been withheld for so long that they worry that the sorrowing will not end. That fear is real and quite common.

Sometimes, when I hear this, I tell them that I will help them end their crying at some point. I won't let them drown in their tears. That's part of the job of a therapist is to help you hold your tears safely.

You can let your counselor know how you feel about tears. Sometimes, it's an entire conversation about what to do when/if tears happen. Those conversations are OK to have.

Other times, when I know the client could use a giggle, I'll ask them about the last time they were in the mall and how many folks they saw weeping as they went about their business because they started to cry and never stopped. People *always* stop crying. Sometimes it just takes a while.

Some client's eyes well up—just a trace. It's like they leak, just a little. Or there can be quiet weeping. Sometimes, people come in and sob. Occasionally there is wailing. It doesn't alarm me. I just pass the tissue. Often, people are surprised by how great they feel after a good cry.

It's a brave thing to enter an internal room full of pain that may have been locked shut for years. When tears happen, it's a sign a person has walked into it and is looking around.

Tears are the brave sign that you have gone to an important and intimidating and powerful place. Yes, you might cry when you see a counselor. Entering a room that is opened by the experience of tears means entering a room that hasn't yet been fully explored.

But if you cry will be courageous like when a Navy SEAL goes into a compound on a reconnaissance mission to explore and discover important information.

And you won't find the SEAL apologizing.

14 The floodgates will open

Picture your soul as a large home with a variety of rooms. Some are sunny and full of life with lots of action, frequent cleaning, holding laughter and good times.

Some rooms are a little dusty with less use, more like rooms that are visited as necessary. The door is shut on these rooms, but the handles can be turned and the rooms entered.

Some rooms are locked and bolted shut, not having been inhabited or even visited for years. They get no light and often are in the basement. If a visitor might ask for on a tour, you wouldn't even acknowledge these rooms exist.

Some of these rooms have dark closets in the back corner with secrets tucked inside that remain firmly locked up.

Maybe you have had some very painful experiences in your life. Experiences that you have put away in a dark closet in your mind because the thought of bringing them out again creates shivers down your spine or nauseous feelings in your belly. Perhaps the death of a parent, the violating touch of a coach/club leader/sibling when you were a child or the shame of a parent's reaction to a school grade or not making the team. The experiences vary but the gut-wrenching sensations associated with those experiences are more similar than alike.

Many spend their lives trying to cloister the painful memories as far away from conscious thought as possible. A belly twitches if a song or a smell has them go there. When they read something online or watch a show where someone experiences something similar to the avoided feelings, they know sleep will go poorly that night.

The body teaches a person to avoid the painful memories that are then kept locked away.

Many shut those parts away because it feels awful to just even feel the slightest initial bit of those memories.

There can be the sense of, "If I feel this bad when I just begin to think of it, how bad would it be if I started talking about it with someone else?" Often people live out of this idea without ever knowing that they have made this choice. The fear of the potential power of exploring these intentionally neglected pieces of ourselves is significant.

To be clear, very few folks say, "I will avoid every circumstance related to my most uncomfortable feelings," to themselves. Your body does it for you, unawares, somewhat like your eyelids blink over your eyes to lubricate them. You are never aware that your eyeballs are becoming dry. Your brain tells your eyelids to blink without conscious awareness that this is a good idea.

And so a person organizes his or her existence to make sure those areas of their lives never get talked about or explored.

- He doesn't watch certain television shows because those shows have a similar theme. Theme avoided—inside pain avoided.

- She mocks certain movies that might have her feel certain feelings. When you mock a movie for its emotional themes, you have an obvious reason to not expose yourself to watching it and to remove the threat of touching on tender spots when the characters struggle with that which you are avoiding.

- He might avoid funerals—or avoids listening to anything at the funeral if he finds himself feeling the real sadness present. He might look like he's there, but he has walled himself off. He sits in the pew, stony. Shut off. Feeling nothing. Because it's safer than feeling the feelings the funeral service would elicit—which are the same feelings he shut down and shut off decades ago when dad died.

- She becomes a cordial roommate with her spouse, because the deeper, more intimate conversations that they once had now become dangerous. The deeper conversations might touch too close to the parts of herself she will never, ever go near. How can she tell him how, sometimes, his touch feels eerily like the unwelcome touch of the man who persuaded her to trust him when she was a child?

❧❧

When a family physician, boss or a dear friend, encourages counseling, it's not uncommon for there to be a lot of bluster. Comments like, "There is no time! Where would I find the time?" or, "Much ado about nothing. I'm not sure what all the fuss is about!" These are fantastic, vague comments to blow someone off who has spent the time thinking about it, and risked suggesting it.

In my experience, when those people somehow make it to counseling, the terrible, terrifying truth comes out: "I have spent years/decades avoiding the experience, memories and feelings around _______ and if I start, I fear I will drown in it. I dare not open the box, because I won't be able to put it back, and it may just finish me."

❧❧

When a person has deliberately spent decades avoiding discussion or even thought of the:

- Sexual assault
- Sudden death of someone significant
- Serious accident
- Experience of war
- Violent relationship
- Abuse by parent or caregiver
- Absentee parent
- Stillbirth

—the idea to go to counseling and explore that space seems ridiculously counterintuitive. As in, why would you put your phone in a blender and turn it on? Why would you walk on thin ice that is cracking? Counterintuitive like snow in July.

There can be a fear of:

- Falling apart and never coming back together
- Starting to cry and never stopping
- Being so concerned about what might happen, that you wonder if spending time with that needs-to-be-ignored space might just kill you.
- Beginning to talk about the one terrible bit of it you remember when you suspect there is more that you can't remember, and you presume that what you can't remember is even worse. You assume these unknown memories would flood you and sink you fast if you opened the door, even just a little. This one is especially terrifying. If you don't know what you don't remember, then you don't know how unspeakably horrendous these pieces of memory could be.

Some of you spend your life making sure that the fragile container holding your most painful moments isn't touched during regular life. Ever.

You avoid the triggers by:

- Not ever visiting that part of town
- Changing the radio whenever a certain song plays
- Shutting off the television when it discusses certain types of news events, or maybe not watching the news at all.
- Changing the conversation
- Never talking to certain kinds of people
- Never letting yourself feel a certain feeling—or even feel anything at all.

If you go to all that work to make certain that fragile container is never touched—then, **why the hell would you go to counseling** if the purpose of that therapy is to tap at that container? What if it shatters into a million pieces that you can never glue back together? And if that container shatters, then whatever-the-heck is in that container is now not contained.

Therapy would seem to be the antithesis of how you organize your life!

So, first of all, no good therapist will recklessly shatter your guarded and protected container that holds your most precious and tender and frightening moments. We don't shatter and crush.

That violates **everything** that a therapist stands for and desires for you.

If a therapist should attempt to push too hard, let them know that this counseling approach will not work.

You can do that. You can say, "Slow down," or "You're pushing too hard," or "I couldn't sleep for days after last session, can we pull back today?" Let the therapist know what pace is tolerable for you. If the therapist doesn't respond well to your concerns, find another therapist who will support even as you explore.

Therapists **do not** smash the container with the avoided memories and feelings.

However, therapists are "professional peekers-into-dark-and-locked-closets".

Counselors have spent years learning how to peek and we know how to help clients peek. Safely.

No one should have to peek into their own deep darkness alone. We peek together with you. Peeking may not be fun. No barrel of laughs here. But it will be tolerable—maybe just barely tolerable. But definitely tolerable.

Peeking isn't pleasant, but it is infinitely more desirable than smashing the container. Peeking into the scary container with a therapist is a similar to entering a bright room when you've been in the dark for days. Your clamp your hands over your eyes. You squint from behind the hands that have two fingers open just a crack. It's so bright it hurts. It isn't easy. You stop squinting and close your eyes until the pain passes.

You pull back when it's hard and regroup. Then you find you can open your eyes a teeny bit more than before, for a minute longer than before. Over time, your eyes adjust. What used to be intolerable, now becomes tolerable. It doesn't hook you or hijack you in the way it used to. When it still comes up in a surprising way and you feel triggered, you have tools to deal with it.

Do you remember Dorothy in the Wizard of Oz?[iii] She is desperate to get home to Kansas. She approaches the Wizard—a terrifying head on a throne, with huge plumes of smoke and periodic burst of huge fire popping out and with a big terrifying booming voice. She is shaking in fear until Toto, her dog, runs behind the curtain and finds a tiny man speaking into a microphone, earnestly pulling and pushing levers. He creates the special effects to present as frightening—because he himself is anxious and frightened. When Dorothy scolds him for going to such great lengths to misrepresent himself in such a terrifying way, she exclaims: "You're a very bad man." It's clear to the viewer that the man makes himself to be much scarier and meaner and bigger and more significant that he is in real life. He operates out of a knowing that that others will not value him as he is. He charmingly discloses, "I'm a very good man, just a very bad wizard."

It's feels vulnerable to become exposed and often those rooms that hold the dark secrets find it to their advantage to become terrifying. Being so intimidating keeps you out of their secrets which are tender and wounded, and fearful of greater hurt. It's a therapist's task to walk with you towards those locked rooms and to approach them carefully and cautiously.

The wounded part of you in the darkened, locked room is more frightened of you than you of it. A therapist holds space with you to gently open that room and is a companion on the way. A therapist creates the safety for both you and for the woundedness locked away, quavering in the dark, convinced that exposing itself will lead to certain judgement and further hurt.

Dorothy walked into the wizard's room with friends. That's an important detail about the story. It was her trusty sidekick, Toto that found the unique angle of the wizard, revealing that he was all smoke and mirrors. Dorothy would not have been able to confront the wizard on her own. She wouldn't have discovered the truth of the wizard on her own. She couldn't have had the experience end well without the courage, support and creativity of her companions.

We all need support, and we aren't meant to go to deepest hidden places inside of ourselves without another to go with us. It's too intimidating to open up long locked up doors into the hidden darkness without another person ready to face the results with you. But even more importantly, going in with another transforms the experience.

Toto pulls back the curtain. Tinman points out the exposed man. Dorothy's experience of approaching the wizard becomes possible because of her allies. She doesn't go alone. They actively involve themselves to help her in the process.

Exploring those dark and hidden inner spaces that are terrifying can shift to become something surprisingly possible. The experience is altered when you have a compassionate, courageous therapist accompanying this expedition.

Often what is behind those locked doors is a wounded, terrified part that is lonely and longs for understanding and compassion. When that part is approached gently and respectfully with a therapist, it drops the smoke and fire, and looks to see if a relationship can might be built. It's fragile and hesitant and it may feel such relief at being allowed out from behind the door. That part may weep the tears of relief and sadness of one that has long waited to be heard and valued. It may express some irritation that it has been long ignored. Wouldn't it be weird if it didn't?

But most of all, the part that was locked away and now released will be relieved to be seen and known.

I'm not asking you to believe me. I'm asking you to find this out for yourself.

15 Therapy is selfish

Navel gazing.

When people are critical of others who gaze at themselves and talk at length about themselves, they use the term *navel gazing*. Some folks that come to therapy come in reluctantly and secretly, knowing that if their friends and family knew, they would be considered navel gazers.

It's a derisive term that is condescending. The implication is a navel gazer is looking at themselves at the expense of others. A navel gazer, metaphorically, is someone fascinated by the lint they find in their belly button.

Nobody wants to be a navel gazer by that definition!

When *the chips are down* and you and yours aren't doing well:

- Your spouse has left and you are frantically trying to parent confused and struggling children on your own
- A close family member has died and you're all struggling
- A child is experimenting with drugs and is not doing well and you exhausted and frantic
- A close friend is playing with death with an eating disorder and her inner turmoil is front and center (and your hidden agony and terror watching this unfold grows by the day)
- You are having flashbacks from childhood abuse as you go about the regular day-to-day work of being a good spouse, productive employee and caring friend
- It can feel like a luxury to go for counseling yourself.

When you're the person who is always making sure everybody else is fed and watered, cared for and feeling loved, it can seem like an unnecessary extravagance to go to a therapist and talk about yourself. When you're struggling because someone you care about is struggling even worse, you seek to focus on the loved one. Getting care because you hurt for another, while the other is swirling around the toilet bowl can *feel* like total navel gazing.

I love to watch cooking shows. Cooking competitions are my favorites. One of the prominent features that I have noticed about chefs is that when they move into a kitchen, they bring their own knives. They carry their knives in a little rolled up satchel. At the onset of the episode, there are often clips of these chefs sharpening their knives (in slow motion, for effect, of course) or carefully gazing at the sharp blade to inspect its quality. They then pull their knives out to cut the vegetables or meat with clean, even and quick cuts.

My husband, Jim, is a carpenter. He builds beautiful things with wood. In the summer, he builds decks and fences. Every morning, he and his crew will arrive at the yard where they are building and set up the table saw, set up the air compressor, plug in the air nailer, and put their drills in their tool belts. Every evening, he and his crew wrap up the cords, and put away their tools for the night. They don't want them to be exposed to the elements or to get stolen. Carpentry tools are essential to Jim's craft.

No tools, *no* carpentry.

Lousy tools, *mediocre* carpentry. As simple as that.

Good tools are important, and craftspeople understand that.

Guess what the primary tool is for you in your relationships?

You.

Yes, you.

I believe that when the going gets rough, and everybody, including you, is struggling, it's not selfish to do your work, ground yourself, and get your head on straight. It's the opposite of selfish. It's brilliant. The smart and caring thing to do is to take proper care of you so you are strong, capable and on your game when all around you is falling apart.

Years ago, as a new single parent, I recall firsthand that there was no time to do anything for myself. By the time I did my job, drove kids around, cleaned house, made meals, did laundry, dealt with the nightmares of children and the upset as they adjusted to going back and forth from one house to another, the day was gone. No time at all. No budget for therapy either since the expenses had increased while the household revenue tanked.

But how is anyone supposed to parent well when grieving the death of a marriage?

When:

- you wake early.
- your heart pounds every time your former spouse's number is on call display
- you have big feelings and judge yourself for those feelings and that becomes a runaway train
- you are figuring out how to live without your partner's support for the first time in many years

— how can anyone provide good care to children?

When, as a parent you spin endlessly about a thousand unknowns, how can you calm and soothe your anxious children?

❧❧

As you seek to be the best mother you can be, the best boss, the best employee, the best friend or spouse or uncle or dad, the way to do it is by recognizing that what you offer to those relationships is you. If you are anxious, depressed, caught up in nasty cycles, or so angry you can't see straight, you offer a version of yourself that isn't fully present. You are highly reactive. You are stressed.

However, if you:

- have a perspective on what is happening and on how it is affecting you

- become aware of your own blind spots
- are resourcing yourself

—then you are in a better position to be compassionate and empathic to those around you.

You will have improved ability to make better choices when asked to do things that may sound helpful, but in reality, are destructive in the situation. You will have a place to be sad, mad, or stressed to enable you to enter a situation and handle the conversations of others that are sad, mad or stressed.

It's important, if you are a caregiver supporting people around you in a time of crisis, to get help for yourself. Often friends, family, and support of social resources will be enough. But sometimes you will recognize that you are not being the best you that you can be in the middle of trying to parent your children, support your elderly parents, or work on a big project at work. You're drowning under the pressures of the current situation, or the past is threatening to swamp you as you deal with the present.

If you're so depressed you can hardly get up in the morning and you are so preoccupied with the sadness in your inner world that there is little interaction with your children or your friends, then they don't get the *you* they need.

If you're so anxious that you can't sit down and enjoy a leisurely conversation with your spouse, then your spouse gets robbed of time with you that you would want to give. If you're so stressed that you can't sleep, and you're exhausted, and you cancel your plans with friends the next day, everybody loses out on enjoying *you*.

It's at those times when care for the caregiver is actually a selfless act.

As you sharpen your own emotional knives, oil the moving parts of your thoughts and tweak and adjust the tool of you in counseling, you will optimize your ability to positively impact those around you.

When a chef sharpens his knives, and Jim spends an hour cleaning up his tools and getting them ready for the next day, they aren't wasting time. They are investing in being able to do a quality job.

When you choose to go to counseling in the middle of a busy and stressful life and people are depending on you, you're not being selfish. You're investing in the most important tool you've got to make a difference in the lives of those you care about—you.

By seeking extra support, you aren't taking away from giving to others. You are adding to your ability to give to others.

By doing your work with a therapist, you are modelling to your family, your friends or your work team that it is a good thing to take care of yourself. You are letting them have the experience of witnessing someone who does good self-care.

What could be a greater lesson for those you care about to learn from you than to learn how to take care of oneself?

16 I'm strong enough to do it on my own

I have long lived in a house full of males growing from fine young boys into better young men. Lots of testosterone. These guys frequently see who is getting taller and stronger and who was taller and stronger at a certain age. They recount their sporting exploits—the stories I hear them share and share again are ones of dominance and victory. They talk about the last-minute basket that they swished, or the way they blocked the other's shot at the buzzer. Not so much now, but they used to wrestle a lot, trying to show the other he was the stronger one. They tell me stories of jumping off the garage roof into the pool or using the garage roof as the beginning of their sledding run. The loved recounting stories of their bravery and courage riding their bikes over rough terrain.

My boys love the stories of athletes who have overcome adversity to show tremendous strength in spirit and body. Clearly, the people—all boys except for me—in my house admire strength and I don't think that's unique to my household.

Don't we all like to be known as capable and strong? There are phrases that, when tossed casually our way, fill a person with shame:

- Why don't you pull yourself up by your own bootstraps?
- Build a bridge and get over it
- Suck it up buttercup
- Don't be such a princess
- Pansy
- Wimp
- Wuss

Strength is a quality long admired in our Western world. Strength as measured by an individual's fortitude in persevering in challenges of all kinds. The concept that "It is me against the world" is a huge challenge for an individual to conquer what lies ahead of them. We prize individual strength in our culture beyond almost anything else. Physical, emotional, psychological strength—all of it.

In our culture, it's bad for everybody, but even a greater sting for men to receive even hints of perceived weakness. Men are supposed to be strong and brave—and *never let'em see you sweat*. There is an unwritten, unspoken expectation that strong men won't seek therapy. There is an implicit understanding that says a strong guy is expected to push through the pain of:

- A still-born child
- A failed thesis
- A broken engagement
- Crippling anxiety
- Trauma brought on by seeing a friend blown up on an Afghani road by an IED

In a world where expressing and exploring emotions is weakness, going to counseling can only be interpreted as a form of emotional and psychological collapse. Starting therapy in a culture that values individual achievement at all costs, is a defeatist act, that says, *"I'm not strong enough"*.

Men who have always prided themselves on their own strength get boxed into a place where asking for help isn't possible. People who have done remarkable things in their lives, who have been heroic and helpful, find themselves in a position of an emotional struggle with little or no option. They dare not let others into their own pain to tarnish their image *of being strong*. The cultural script says that *real men don't go to therapy*. (And strong women may not find it such a good idea either if they want to keep up with the boys.)

This cultural narrative is unspoken but runs very deep. There is concern about prospects of future career opportunities lost if clients would ever have to disclose attendance at therapy. Men are often sheepish when they show up for a first appointment. They have only come after a long period of their spouse's encouragement and are hesitant to be seen as a failure if they attend counseling.

Let me say two things about strength and then I will unpack each one of them:

1. Brute strength is not helpful in many situations. Often qualities other than strength are more valuable.
2. There are different ways of understanding and viewing strength.

The first idea: strength, either physically or emotionally, isn't always helpful. How well does brute strength work to:

- Force a thread through the eye of a needle?
- To make a child stop crying by ordering them to cheer up?
- Defuse a bomb by smashing it?
- Fix a computer by kicking it?
- Remove a brain tumor by carving a hole in a person's brain and just cutting it out?

Raw strength *is* helpful:

- In opening a pickle jar
- Hammering nails into wood
- Lifting a car that has a person under it

—and a host of other situations.

There are, however, many situations where strength gets you nowhere. Circumstances where using strength is counterproductive and will break, rupture, destroy and just plain not work. Surgeons, architects, chefs, artists, accountants, information technology engineers and so many other professions rely on artful technique and careful finesse to get the job done. There may be moments requiring strength, but even very physical jobs still require decision making, planning, strategy, attention to detail, analysis and so on. Strength a very important component of success in a lot of tasks— but *only one* of many very important factors.

It's fair to say the physically strongest physicians are not the best doctors and the strongest woodworkers do no craft the most beautiful furniture. Being the strongest doesn't produce excellence in most tasks.

Even jobs requiring brute strength often also require many other elements to facilitate the success of the task. Digging a ditch, for example, requires creating the correct path and depth, using the right tools for this particular ditch with this soil. If they use a mechanical assist like a front-end loader, finesse at the controls is infinitely more useful than raw strength.

Strength, while valuable, seems to be an odd characteristic for Western society to value above all others.

The second idea: Is there a different way of understanding strength?

I went to the memorial service of my husband Jim's late wife, Car. She was a friend of mine. I hardly knew him then. The large church was packed with friends, colleagues, classmates of her sons and so on. At the onset of the service, the hundreds of us in the pews of that church rose in silent vigil, as the family filed in behind the pastor and walked to the front.

Can you imagine the strength required to walk into the service? As hundreds of people looked on, Jim and his sons lined up with Car's sisters and her mother to walk down the aisle.

It was painful to watch them file in, feeling their agony. The collective audience could readily acknowledge the raw strength required to be grieving, and yet so present publicly. They were emotionally vulnerable and yet were visible to honor the life of the woman whom they loved so dearly.

I remember watching Jim walk to the pulpit in the large sanctuary and to speak to us about his wife. He talked about her—what he loved about her, what he would miss, what he hoped his children would remember about her and carry on as her legacy. He stood up and began to speak in front of hundreds of people. He didn't know how he would do, if he would cry or not, if he would remember his speech at such an emotional time. He took the risk and showed up. He honored his wife in incredible ways.

I remember thinking that for him to take such risks, to be bold when he was so very vulnerable was so very strong.

It takes strength to:

- Cry when you are not known to be a crier.
- Tell a story of how someone hurt you as a child when you have never dared to unpack that story
- Explore a painful feeling when you have never wrapped language around it before.
- Trust a therapist who is working with you when you have never had this conversation before with anybody.

Don't let anybody tell you it doesn't take strength to turn to your wife and tell her how scared you are to lose her. It's a real strength to let your your son know you love him when you've never dared tell him before. It's a mighty strength needed to be vulnerable and show tender spots that you regularly keep hidden.

It takes strength to let someone in. It takes strength to be vulnerable and connect with another. That strength is something I admire. And I get to witness that kind of fortitude regularly.

It never gets old to watch. Often, after I witness that sort of courage, and the person walks down the hall after that session, and I hear the door close, I will exclaim: "I love being a therapist!" Because having a front-row seat to that style of strength and courage is a privilege to witness. It makes me a stronger and better person myself.

Section IV Real reasons to Choose Counseling

It's a lot easier to put up reasons you should **not** do something than to speak effectively **for** something. People can easily complain about the problems. It's more challenging to speak positively about constructive solutions.

When you ask someone if they are interested in going to therapy, they can give you a half dozen reasons why it makes sense not go. Some might feel like *reasons*, while others will actually be excuses. We've looked at both reasons and excuses to avoid therapy.

If you ask a person for the rationale for choosing therapy, they will have more of a challenge. It's hard to explain why, at some level, it makes sense to bare the parts of your soul that, mostly, you choose not to expose to others.

I was at a banquet last month and I met a fellow. We introduced ourselves. Once he heard my name, he confirmed that I was "the Carolyn Klassen" from Conexus Counselling. Then he told me that his brother was a client of mine years ago and that his brother had often recited a line from a counseling session to himself over the years, as a lifeline to reassure himself. The fellow could easily recite this line, having heard his brother declare it repeatedly. I don't remember saying it, but it sounded like something I might have said.

The memory of a moment in a session, long forgotten by me, had helped him through a tough season.

❧

Early in my years as a therapist, I was finishing a course of therapy with a client. She was one of the first clients with whom I was ending therapy. She had reached the goals we had set when she first came, and now we were just wrapping up.

I was feeling rather proud of myself as a new therapist. She had done so well, and I asked her what she took from the sessions. What would she remember? Was it one of my brilliant insights, a clever comment, a wonderful reframe on my part? What about therapy had made the difference?

She responded that she had the feeling in her body during therapy sessions like she felt when she was with her grandma—a warm, safe, secure feeling. She had forgotten about that feeling, and it was good to feel it again.

Oh, and she also *walked taller* now. That *feeling taller* as she moved through about her world changed everything, although she couldn't put her finger on why that shift had happened. She just knew that it had developed over the sessions and that she was grateful. It changed how she talked to people and that changed how people responded to her.

❧

There's *no telling* what will happen when you go to therapy or how it

- could change the way you see yourself or the world
- will change the way you feel your feelings, or think your thoughts
- will shift the manner in which you move about the world
- could transform your relationships in terrifyingly beautiful ways

But I can tell you how it has impacted others.

Let's review why people show up for therapy.

17 To get the bottom and deal

The landlord kept telling us, each time we called to express our concern, variations of the following:

- There are no external cracks in the building's foundation
- If it was the window that was leaking, it would run down the drywall of the office underneath the window. The wall is dry, so it's not the window.
- I've walked around the outside of the building after a heavy rain, and there isn't a standing water issue outside of the building.

The implication was that if there wasn't a clear source for leaking into our basement offices, then the wet carpets against the outside wall were probably a figment of our imagination.

With no apparent and obvious deficiency, the floor couldn't possibly be wet with a leak or so management said. But the carpet was wet annually in spring during the snowmelt and sometimes after a torrential rain.

This spring, I was done. Exasperated, I urged the building manager to come in and look at the wet spots again. We had put our wooden furniture up on blocks semi-permanently to prevent damage.

I expressed my concern again. This time they tacked the issue head on—I don't know why they did something this year, but I'm relieved. It would be a lot of effort and inconvenience, but we would figure this out.

There were some empty offices down the hall, and we moved our furniture to the temporary location to let them figure this out properly. We made plans to be out of the offices for several weeks. My sweet family hauled all the furniture from two therapy offices into some temporary office space down the hall and into the vacant office space that was always dry. We put up signs for the clients, apologizing for the disruption and hoped they would be understanding.

The first step the landlord did was to take off the bottom two feet of sheetrock on the outside wall. He did so just underneath the window on the wall next to where the wet carpet always developed—about 6 feet wide.

Nothing showed up.

The now-exposed insulation and all the construction material looked immaculate. No problem was apparent. The landlord didn't say it explicitly, but I got the impression that he believed there was actually no problem. Was it all in our head?

(Except it was also on our wet socks.)

I wondered if they thought I was pouring jugs of water on the carpet near the wall.

Then the Concrete Expert Guy (CEG) came. The landlord, the CEG and I looked at the wall and talked at length. CEG was clear there was no way to discern what the issue was by removing only the bottom couple of feet of sheet rock just under the window. He told us he wanted to investigate his way. We gave him the green light.

CEG took down the bottom 6 feet of the wall all across the entire room. Then he pulled back the plastic vapour barrier and the pink insulation and called us back in to look.

Now it was obvious.

Now it was clear. There was a modest crack in the concrete wall. The concrete was below ground level so when the ground was saturated, the water came through the crack in the concrete, soaking the insulation and the studs. When it was wet enough, the moisture would dribble to the basement floor level and soak the carpet, creeping across the room.

When CEG reached to touch the studs with his hands to demonstrate the damage, the rotten wood crumbled. It disintegrated in his hand. The pink insulation adjacent to the wall was black with mold, with bits and pieces stuck to the wall because of the long-standing moisture. Pieces of stud had fallen off.

It was a concealed and undetected mess. But just because we couldn't see it, didn't mean it wasn't affecting us from time to time with wet carpet. It was potentially impacting us all the time from molding and rotting substances.

This time, instead of using fans, dehumidifiers and carpet cleaning on the problem, CEG injected a substance into the crack. When the substance came in contact with the moisture in the crack, it expanded and then dried, creating a watertight seal. Then he:

- reinstalled the studs
- put new insulation in place
- then vapor barrier
- installed sheet rock
- applied dry wall tape, mudded and sanded it smooth.

Finally, they painted. The whole process took weeks.

We were camping out in the down-the-hall offices for more than a month.

It was a *huge* hassle for therapists and clients alike to be out of our usual space for sessions. After a session, we had to go back to the administration portion of our office for the paperwork and payment. **But it was worth it.**

What we were doing *behind* the walls of the therapy room to stop the recurring intermittent wet carpet is what our clients are doing *within* the walls of the therapy room. Every day, the clients within the walls of that office work at what we were doing to repair those very walls: going deep to fix it.

As humans, our first response is to judge a situation just by its surface—if there is no obvious problem, we breathe a sigh of relief and move on. If others can't see an obvious issue, then we just wish it away. If it's not obvious to others, maybe it doesn't exist.

Even if underneath there are problems with rotting and erosion—and sometimes there are signs something serious is occurring—we just want to ignore the situation and desperately hope it won't bring us down.

Our clients do the difficult and brave work to figure stuff out. They choose to stop pretending it's not a problem. Clients in therapy stop denying the way they hurt themselves and others. They launch out to find the true story and to write a different ending. Clients in therapy tackle their stories at their source to allow them to write different ones. The pain and dysfunction stop dribbling into their lives at the most inconvenient moments because they source the root of the issue and address it.

Our clients get brave.

In counseling, our clients get curious.

They dig deep and they get powerful.

They don't just accept the status quo as good enough.

- He doesn't just accept that his withdrawal from his wife is just because there is a big project at the office. He's been busy with "the next project" for 15 years. Working hard is a good cover for whatever reason stops him from relaxing and spending quality time with his family. For years, even he wasn't aware that he worked that hard not only to make his boss happy, but because it worked at a deeper level for him. But his boss is now taking vacations because of a newfound appreciation for family after the *wake-up call* of his own father's death. He knows he could just keep working the hours he is working with the same reasons of projects and deadlines as he always has. But his doctor is encouraging him to slow down because his blood pressure is borderline high. Now he is ready to figure out what stops him from planning family vacations and being home in time for dinner a few times per week.

- She isn't content to continue to avoid dinners with girlfriends, outings with her husband, and functions of all occasions. If she's honest, she doesn't want to feel that uncomfortable feeling that she might do or say something embarrassing in a social setting. She is tired of staying at home to avoid all conversation of real life, knowing that she lives her life small and tries nothing new. That feeling of anxiety is well hidden when she is watching Netflix. It doesn't look like anything is hugely wrong because she is just living a quiet life. Once you say "no" often enough, people stop asking, and so nobody even notices that she avoids social situations. However, she is bored silly and wants to start living.

- He's done with walking away from situations because that's the only way he knows not to let his rage explode in ways that could end relationships or be criminal. Walking away prevents the explosions. When conversations get tense, the alarm goes off inside of him. He knows if he doesn't get out of there, he will blow. So, he walks away. His wife wonders if he cares, because of the way he seems to blank out whenever the conversation gets serious and he leaves mid-conversation. His kids are convinced he doesn't love them when they are upset. He cares deeply, of course, except that no one would even know because of his frequent departures in the middle of meaningful conversations. This pattern has taught them to only talk about sports scores (though never with high stakes play-off games), the weather, and *good news* stories of great school tests and funny videos on social media. It might not appear like there is a problem to the outside eye. However, his children don't confide in him and his wife sees him more like a roommate than an intimate partner. He's wanting to dig into this pattern and figure out how to stay engaged in important conversations, even when he starts to feel angry.

They're digging deep to discover the root of the problem and deal with it once and for all. Clients who go to therapy aren't willing to mop up the damage and hope it goes away anymore. Clients in therapy recognize that it's a hassle to look for the source of the problem. They also appreciate that, in the long run, this creates a situation where repeated issues don't keep re-occurring.

We love being back in our offices, this time with walls that won't leak, and carpets that will stay dry.

Being curious about what is behind the walls in your life pays off. It's creates a disturbance to dig deep and get curious. It's definitely an inconvenience to:

- look at what is causing the shame
- work through the grief

- to find out in what ways you have been restricting healthy behaviors

It's also a challenge to give yourself permission to create shifts within yourself. To talk about matters of the heart is an aggravation. But to process your stuff is profoundly helpful in moving forward without having to work around the recurring issues.

At least, that's what our clients have told us.

18 We all need a safe place to connect

For the first five or six years of my private practice, I had therapy sessions with clients in a windowless office. I put a large and beautiful picture of the outdoors in the room above the loveseat as a pseudo-window to brighten up the space.

It wasn't just any picture. It was a special gift from my husband-at-the-time who knew how much I liked California scenery. We spent two wonderful years studying during the week and exploring the California sights and scenery on the weekends. We loved the coast of California, walking the boardwalks and the piers. Clam chowder in a sourdough bread bowl was a splurge that we would make on those weekends. We couldn't really afford that soup (and the chocolate-covered caramel apple for dessert) on our student budget, and I still don't have any regrets on that splurge. That soup in the sea air tasted like something they serve in heaven. We went to see a taping of The Price is Right in Los Angeles and let the sea lions entertain us in San Francisco. Both were free and fit in our budget just fine.

But it was the sequoias that took my breath away. They were an hour's drive away from grad school. One regret I have is that we didn't drive up to the forest more often. I loved to be in the sequoia forest.

Seriously, sequoia trees are remarkable. They are the largest living things on this whole earth of ours. Gigantic. The California Redwoods often get the sexy press because they are taller—but because of their diameter, the sequoias win the prize for the largest for sheer mass.

My husband-at-the-time, knowing how special our time in California was for me, and how much I loved those trees. He purchased a poster 8 feet long and 3 feet tall of the forest and had it mounted as a piece of art that could hang in my office. Sometimes I looked up and away from the client to prepare a thoughtful response and that poster of sequoia trees was what I saw in that moment:

I loved the idea of sequoia trees in the counseling office. I'll confess a slight addiction to metaphors—a common issue for therapists. It often works to draw connections between the world we live in and the things we are processing in therapy. I love a beautiful metaphor and the sequoia tree represents a powerful message for me. In fact, the richest lesson on relationships didn't happen in the classroom during those years but in the forest—amongst the sequoias. They taught me so much it became a TEDx Winnipeg talk in 2018[iv]

Sequoias are this incredible mix of power and beauty. You can drive a truck through the hollows of a trunk. They are amongst the oldest living things on earth. Incredible and majestic. They are also fragile.

These gigantic trees have shallow root systems. Sequoias can extend 20-25 stories tall. Remarkably, their roots are within 4-5 feet from the surface. Can you imagine? A 250-foot structure that can weigh 12 million pounds and have been standing for two millennia has roots that go into the ground not even as far as the height of an adult.

We found when we went to visit the sequoias that most of them have large fences around them, preventing people from trampling or wearing down the ground around the bases of the trees. As mighty as they are, they have extremely fragile root systems.

The sequoia trees have this incredible, intricate combination of strength and vulnerability.

Just like our clients.

Our clients demonstrate this incredible strength in saying, "I will talk about the parts of me that, because I'm avoiding, now control me as I endeavor to pretend they aren't there." When I see clients share their story in all its raw realness, it takes my breath away.

Let me give you one more fascinating fact about the sequoias that helps me understand the value of counseling. There is a reason these enormous trees have stood the test of time over thousands of years. They have stood tall even with the worst of whatever California storms could throw at them. There is an important reason why these trees with shallow and vulnerable root systems have survived for hundreds, even thousands of years. **They grow near each other.**

The root systems, which spread out 150-200 feet, and can cover an acre, intertwine with the root systems of neighboring trees. In weaving together with the roots of other neighboring trees, they give each other strength, support and stability. It is through the interconnection with one another that sequoias continue to thrive.

In effect, these *sequoias are strengthened by living in community.*

Just like our clients.

We are wired for connection. For several years, I have had a half hour gig on a popular talk radio show every week. The host will interview me about a particular topic which we decide the night before. Pretty much each week, as part of explaining forgiveness, jealousy, anxiety or stress, the radio listeners will hear me say, "We are wired for connection." It comes up as significant in almost every topic that the host, Hal Anderson, invites this therapist to talk about. The drive to be connected to others is innate to all of us.

❧

Picture this. Two hundred years ago there was no television. Supplies like books, games, and paper and pencil existed, but were not as plentiful as today. Electric power wasn't common, and lights weren't as bright as today. No computers, no movie theatres—no screens of any kind. A lot of the activities that take up most of our time now didn't exist then.

Transportation was different, too. No airplanes. No cars. Travel was by horse and buggy. Most people lived their entire lives within a few miles of where they were born. Some might travel a long distance, but even then, would settle down. Travel was slower, more difficult and more dangerous than it is now. Moving might happen once in a lifetime.

Lifestyles were very different back then. Most folks lived a stable rural life. The agrarian lifestyle meant that often multiple generations lived on the same farmyard, and adult brothers/cousins/aunts lived at the next farmyard over.

People lived their lives with more stable connections than they do now, with more hours in the day to invest in those relationships that existed for their entire lives. Life was different.

Imagine a young husband sitting in the barn waiting for his cow to calve. Maybe the cow is having trouble, and he calls his uncle to sit with him so he can learn how to birth this calf when it's time. They sit on bales of hay in the stall with the cow as she labors, maybe for hours. Perhaps all night. To pass the time, in between periods of silence, or a check on the cow, they visit. They've known each other since the young man was a child.

They talk about the weather, the cows, the crops—and over the hours, the conversation deepens. The young husband confides in his uncle that marriage is harder than he thought it would be. The cow has not yet given birth, so they have more hours to converse. Gradually, the younger man opens up about the difficulties he is having and how it seems his wife pushes him away. The uncle can hear him and reminisces aloud about his own early years of marital adjustments. The young man becomes more reassured about how some struggles are part of normal adjustment. He also gets feedback from his uncle about how he sometimes comes across harsher than he intends. The uncle further talks about what he thinks is important for women to hear and feel in the relationship.

Later in the week, this young man's wife begins to bake some buns and remembers that she has run out of yeast. She goes over to the next farm to borrow some yeast since the store takes a couple of hours to get to, even with the horse-drawn wagon. Once there, the neighbor delights to see a friendly face. She invites her in for tea. They have a visit. They discuss the need to help each other out, using it as an excuse to visit. Helping each other out with supplies and having a visit is part of the beauty of this life. As the visit progresses, she tells this neighbor about her household, managing as a new wife in her own home. After a caring question by the neighbor, she acknowledges that she cowers in light of her husband's pushiness. He is loud and brash and she comes from a household that speaks gently. He intimidates her. The neighbor gently knowingly chuckles, knowing how soft-spoken this young wife's father has always been. She remembers out loud what being newly married was like for her in adjusting to a new family. The neighbor reminds the young woman about her ability to speak up and say what works for her. The neighbor reminds her who she is and empowers her to give feedback to her husband about how she experiences him.

This conversation happens because of hours spent together with someone that a person knows and trusts. The two women trust each other, having developed their relationship over time. Through the mundane connections that happened repeatedly over time with the same few people, one or two showed wisdom and spoke into difficult situations kindly and boldly. She knew who didn't gossip. He could recall how the last time a confidence was shared, it went well. There was time to ease into delicate subjects and conversations could last well past when the candle burnt out or the tea got cold.

You can safely say that I'm idealizing the difficult lifestyle of living on a farm a few generations ago. I will take the criticism. Small communities of years ago likely got into each other's business rather like an old-fashioned soap opera. Folks worked from sun up to sun down before falling into bed exhausted and quite possibly hungry. I don't mean to romanticize the culture as being all, *Little House on the Prairie.*

However, generations ago, relationships were fewer, people depended on each other more for the heavy labor of the time, and there were fewer distractions. People's leisure time was time spent with one other. The foundation was laid for deeper relationships over a lifetime of contact. When crisis hit, you were surrounded by people who knew you and loved you even if they didn't like you.

These days, you may have just moved to the city and no one person has earned the right to hear the heaviness of how hard the move has been for you. No one would understand how the losses of the move remind you of significant past events in your life because they weren't there. You and your family may interact with lots of people all day long—coworkers, coffee shop buddies, fellow soccer parents at the sidelines, strangers in the grocery store—but you lack the deep friendships that come over years of time and conversation.

The sequoia trees do best with multiple other sequoias around, ready to intertwine and weave their roots between others for stability. They do best in a sequoia forest, surrounded by other trees also looking around to be with others. The giant sequoias always grow in a grove.

I'm convinced human beings are a lot like sequoias. We do better when we can intertwine our lives with other human beings. The science is overwhelming: we are healthier, have better quality of life and live longer when we have meaningful connection with others.[v] Deep interwoven connection creates a stability by having others invest in us, allowing us to be vulnerable, and creating opportunities for us to invest in them by deeply hearing their stories.

When folks are transplanted from one city to another, or one lifestyle stage to another, or even one job to another, the stability found in intertwining lives is lost. A fast-paced lifestyle that doesn't allow for the development of relationships can leave a person floundering. When life hands them difficult circumstances, they require the depth of human connection. What happens when no one can provide that connection?

Perhaps our culture allows you to have the *illusion* of many relationships. Many of you say hello to and exchange pleasant banter about the weather and the local sports team. You don't even notice that these relationships are without substance and depth until your back is against the wall. When she walks out the door, or the boss tells you to suddenly pack up your desk, or your child is on life support—only then do you realize that you don't have a relationship that can bear the weight of the pain.

When a crisis hits—mental illness, job loss, marital instability—there is flailing and thrashing with a desperate desire to pour out one's heart.

In a crisis, the need to intertwine your roots with someone else's becomes as necessary as breathing.

We need others all the time.

To be alive is to need to be connected to others.

Often, we become acutely aware of the benefit of being a tree in the forest of other trees when life gets challenging. We yearn to gain strength from another, to lean on another for support. We need to be needed and we need others.

We need that support not because we are weak, but because we are human. Perhaps you, in our world today, suddenly find yourself without others around you. While people abound, none are truly in a position to intertwine their roots with yours. You have no people around able to give you the real support that is vital.

A counselor is not just a therapist, but a fellow tree in the forest of humanity. A therapist has training in providing solid roots to be intertwined, even when meeting with a client for the first time.

Even before our training and expertise, counselors are fellow citizens of the human race, ready to be someone to provide stability in the hearing of a story when no one else feels safe enough. A therapist provides a safe, neutral, confidential space that can hold the pain and terror of a situation that threatens to knock you over. A therapist listens carefully, hears your situation deeply, and begins the worthwhile work with you of figuring out how to move forward. Your roots can intertwine with the counselor's for a time, to give you the stability you need.

A therapy session certainly uses the professional skills of a therapist. But primarily, it is a human encounter where professional boundaries create an inherent safety. The therapist is someone who will sit attentively for the hour to explore your world with you. He or she will keep the conversation private. You can share the story of the painful situation knowing the therapist can handle whatever horrors the story may contain. S/he won't change the subject or give you cheap advice.

In a world where no single other person alive is able to sit with you in a painful darkness, a therapist is able and willing to bear witness to your words, your experience and your feelings. Somehow, a story seems more real when spoken out loud. Putting your experience into words, out loud, in the presence of another human being for the first time, changes it in powerful ways.

Therapy is a place to practice root intertwining again, or perhaps for the first time. And just like the sequoias, you'll be stronger as you intertwine your lives with others and often, a therapist is the best place to start.

19 To stop one problem that was created when fixing another problem

For years, as a single mom, I was the holder of all the keys. The keys to our house, the garage, my bike, multiple keys for each of the three workplaces I worked in, and the car. I lose things like keys easily, so I have all my keys on a carabiner which I loop onto the strap of my purse. Or rather, I *used* to have all my keys on a single carabiner. Let me explain.

Years ago, I was driving an old green Chevrolet Cavalier. She had lots of miles on her, but she was reliable and faithful. I live in a cold climate and a car that starts reliably in winter is something for which to be very grateful.

One day in the fall on my way to the clinic, the key **wouldn't move** in the ignition. It wouldn't budge. It was as though I put the wrong key in the ignition, so it wouldn't do anything at all when I tried to turn it.

I had it towed to the mechanic because it wouldn't start. He took the key I gave him and it started instantly. He started that car ten times in rapid fire, and it started every time. No problem.

Don't you just hate that when it happens? When something that isn't working for you performs like a charm in front of the expert?

It worked fine for a few weeks and then happened again. This time I could eventually get it started and I took it to the mechanic. He took my keys and tried it again. Thankfully, the second time he tried it, it stuck a little. The mechanic mentioned in passing that it seemed sometimes the tumblers in the steering column might have trouble lining up and they might need a little tap or jiggle to fall into place.

As cars age, we expect their little quirks and eccentricities to happen more often. I wasn't surprised when the ignition locking happened more often and was grateful to now have the tool of *tapping* the steering column.

Only sometimes, the *tapping* seemed akin to *hitting*. Sometimes repeatedly. Sometimes my hand would hurt from repeated aggressive, ahem, *tapping* on the steering wheel to get the car so that the key would finally turn and start the car. Once I got the key turning, the car still started like a charm.

One day, to save my hand from the trauma of pounding the steering column, I grabbed the hairbrush in the console beside me. It saved my hand and allowed for even more vigorous banging on that steering column. I started to leave early to allow time for the hair brush whacking. The routine smashing of the steering column started to become part of my lifestyle. As I approached my Chevie, I often began to sing a song in my head my children had often watched on video: "Oh, where is my hairbrush?"[vi]

Fall progressed into winter, and on a bitterly cold day, when I went to start my car, it wouldn't start. The strange situation was that the key turned easily back and forth in the ignition but now the engine wouldn't start.

In the northern climate where I live, our *go to* assumption is that the battery is dead because of the cold. So, I called the local Automobile Association to ask for a *battery boost*. Because of all the others needing a battery boost on that frigid afternoon, it was more than a two hour wait.

Eventually he came, and I explained my plight. He tried to start the car, and he wasn't convinced that it was the battery. He asked permission to try one other strategy first. I consented. What he did next seemed like some weird car voodoo.

He held out his hand for the key and inserted it into the driver's side door. He turned the key to the left as far as it would go and held it there while he counted to ten a slow drawl. Then he turned the key as far right as possible and again held it for a slow count of ten. Then he repeated this odd key dance twice more.

Have I mentioned it was brutally cold out? We were both standing there bouncing up and down trying to stay warm during this slow and seemingly pointless process. I wanted him to boost my battery and get out of there! To spend more than a minute working the key in the car door seemed ridiculous when it was the car's engine that wouldn't start.

However, after he completed what seemed like some slow magical key dance ceremony in the car door, he got in the car, put the key in the ignition and turned. And don't you know, that old green Chevy started like a charm. Even in the bitter, brutal cold.

I was flabbergasted.

He explained that the weird slow and hold key turning ritual in the car door was to reset the car's anti-theft system. He asked me, "Is there any reason your vehicle would think someone had stolen it, and therefore shouldn't start?"

Totally innocently, I was adamant that no one had stolen the vehicle, there had been no danger to the vehicle, and I hadn't a hot clue about why my old green car would think anyone stole it.

I drove off to complete my day, having missed the doctor's appointment, but able to get supper on the table. Better something than nothing, right?

The next day, I put the key into the ignition and it was stuck—wouldn't turn, at all. Motionless. So—I grabbed the hairbrush and started my steering-column-whacking routine. As I assaulted the steering wheel, the lightbulb in my brain suddenly went on bright and bold.

There was good reason for this car to believe someone was trying to steal it. I chuckled when I connected my hairbrush pummeling and the car believing it was being stolen. Now it became obvious.

A week later, my son called me stating that he was turning the key in the ignition and nothing was happening. As a new driver, he didn't know what to do and he did what all boys do when their car doesn't start—he called his momma! I told him to take a deep breath and gave him instructions. I asked him to turn the key all the way one way and hold for 10 seconds, then all the way the other way for 10 seconds and repeat 3 times. I told him not to ask questions but to just do it. Then I told him to start the engine and call me back.

He didn't respond much, but even over the phone, I could tell he thought I was crazy. He called me back two minutes later. It's rare that a momma can impress her adolescent son but I pulled it off on this one! He was astonished at my ability to give him such unusual and yet entirely effective instruction to get the car started when it wasn't working.

I enjoyed the adoration for a few minutes and then told him the truth.

We fixed the problem of the tumblers in the ignition by whacking it so hard that the car comes to think it's stolen.

We fixed one problem, but our strategy to fix it created another.

Our hair brush banging worked—but only partially. Now the car wouldn't start for a reason that we created when all we were trying to do was start the car.

Ironic, huh?

❧

I was at a friend's house a week later, and I was telling my buddy, Dave, about my Cavalier's starting issue. I was at the door getting ready to leave as I was relating my story. I often use my hands to talk and this time was no exception. I had my keys in my hand as I was telling the story. My hand started mimicking the motion that the Automobile Association fellow used when he turned the key back and forth in the car door.

Dave looked at me as I was telling the story and he interrupted me at this point and asked me, "Carolyn, do you put your car key in the ignition with all those other keys attached to it?"

"Hmmm—yes, doesn't everybody keep their keys together and start the car with their key?" I answered.

"Carolyn," he said gently, "You have a lot of keys on your key chain. A **lot** of keys. And it's heavy. When you put your car key in the ignition, it can't go in straight and neutral, where it needs to go. There's so much weight on the key chain. It pulls the car key down when you put it in the ignition, so it goes in at an angle. That could mess with the tumblers inside the ignition."

"Oh," I whispered. I was speechless.

That made sense.

The next day, I bought a second carabiner so that the car, house, and bike lock key were on one loop, and all the work keys were on a second loop. I snapped them together. From then on, to start the car, I would unhook the much smaller, lighter set of keys and insert the car key into the ignition to start the key.

The effective, long lasting, solution that actually addressed the problem of starting my car was far different from the one I had used and felt had worked.

❧❧

So often, when people come to counseling, it is because they want to stop a certain behavior. It's the equivalent of not wanting to keep banging on the steering column with a hairbrush. For example, a person may want to:

- stop procrastinating with college course work
- stop letting their boss walk all over them
- be more open to intimacy with their partner
- be more comfortable with their in-laws
- curb spending on foolish purchases
- be gentler with their children

The dilemma is that the *problem behavior* is actually, at a deep level, working *for* them.

The dysfunctional behavior is needed. People *need* to do those painful, hurtful behaviors **more** than they *don't need* to do them.

Often people are not aware of how the "problem behavior" is actually, at a deep level working for them. This behavior needs to exist because it addresses an issue in their life. Let me give you some examples:

- Procrastinating at school work is possibly a way for a college student to tell one's parents. "I don't like this program and I don't want to be here," may be too difficult to speak directly to her parents who clearly expect her to graduate from college. Her behavior states her reluctance.
- Letting the boss walk all over him is one way he can avoid conflict. Given the meaning he assigns to conflict, he avoids it at

all costs. He is passive in situations, even when people take advantage.

- A person is struggling with anxiety. He drinks several gin and tonics each evening to quiet the inner cacophony. This is successful in calming him, even as it silences his conversations with family. It distances the problems—but it distances everything good in his life as well.

Just as I was unaware that I was fixing one problem and creating another, clients aren't aware that what they are doing to help themselves in one area creates another issue. They have one undesired behavior that addresses a need or desire they are not possibly aware of. This isn't manipulation. This is being alive.

I believe that each person is doing the best they can. When a client comes in desperate to change, I believe there is a part of them that earnestly desires change. I also believe that there is another part of themselves that they are not aware of, that needs that behavior.

When an adolescent looks around and perceives that the world doesn't value them as they are, an eating disorder is a very helpful strategy to:

1. Get thinner. In a world that values thinness as a sign of virtue and beauty, losing weight fast is one strategy to increase their value to the world.
2. Punish themselves for being unlovable. It's distressing to feel devalued, and when a teen perceives him or herself as lacking value and therefore, struggling, it makes sense to make oneself pay for being so worthless.
3. Rally support and care for themselves. As others see an adolescent lose weight or witness signs of an eating disorder, the need for help becomes obvious.
4. Shake up the family. When a child has an eating disorder, parents notice. And care. Parents who are preoccupied with too much work or too much arguing, or worried about money or the child's grades now become focused on the child. This focus on the child's eating can help other members of the family refocus away from something destructive *or*

5. Any number of other reasons it makes more sense to have an eating disorder than not have it.

To be clear, I'm **not** suggesting that *anybody* wakes up one morning and says to him or herself: "Gee, I have a problem here, and I think an eating disorder is a good way to solve it."

Nobody does this on purpose. This is **not** a conscious process. That's why therapy is so necessary to sort the issues out and untangle the confusing knots of pain. And sorting it out is essential because each person is unique. The factors beyond the person's awareness that make the painful behavior understandable will be unique to each client.

I could lighten the weight of the key chain that had my car key on it to allow it to work better once I understood that was a problem.

Similarly, once a client understands the hidden dynamic that perpetuates the "problem behavior", that dynamic can be addressed:

- The recurring nightmare of a survivor of sexual abuse stops once she realizes that the bad dreams are her body's way of telling her that the abuse mattered. She creates a piece of art that speaks of the pain and struggle of the abuse and the innocence of the child she was when it occurred. She hangs it in her house as a reminder of the abuse that occurred. The nightmares subside.

- The anxiety that expresses itself by incessant tidying and needing an immaculate house is discovered to be related to his chaotic childhood. He recalls how his mother said to him, "You will always be as messed up as this house is". He does some work around the power of his mother's words, but now he can make different choices. Much to his wife's relief, he begins to successfully practice leaving an item or two lying around for a day or so.

- A mother realizes that she screams at her toddler because she needs the toddler's behavior to be of a certain high quality to prove her value as a mother. She realizes that she is also very hard on herself as she parents this child. She says out loud to the child the same things she says internally to herself. If she is going to be mean to herself that way, her child deserves the same. Further, this child needs to get ready for when she does this to herself as she gets older. Therapy focuses on how hard she is on herself. She learns to speak with gentleness to herself. As she does so, she yells less at her toddler.

Therapy is a great idea for you if you are doing something you don't like doing but feel powerless to stop it. If you work to change your behavior, but find yourself slipping back, it may be helpful to explore how this behavior is helpful for you at a level you can't yet understand.

20 When *stop gaps* stop working

Years ago, when I took a shower, I got immense satisfaction that immediately after I turned the water off, the tub was empty and glistening. It was a hard-earned beauty. I realize that, normally, a shiny tub is not something in which most people take immense pride. But I have reason to be proud. I have long hair. (Fair warning: these next couple of paragraphs may not be for the squeamish). When I wash my hair, inevitably, individual strands are shed, and make their way towards the drain. Some time ago, the water was increasingly slow to drain. Recognizing the hair issue, I unscrewed the top plug and with tweezers, I pulled this disgusting blob of hairy yuck up and threw it away.

It drained a little better—for a short while. And then it would happen again.

I deliberately clean out from just under the plug regularly. I would unscrew the plug and use tweezers to pull out ugly blob of hair yuck.

Rinse and repeat.

Regular maintenance and effort—I thought that would cure the problem.

I thought wrong.

It's an unfortunate thing, really, when the tub doesn't drain quickly. When the water sits in the tub for a while, soap scum and other gross stuff builds up around the tub. (I told you this part wasn't for the faint of heart). I didn't have the time or energy to give the tub a full scrub every time after anybody in the household showered. I took to keeping the shower curtain closed to hide the ugly effect during the week.

I had to do something. Hiding seemed a reasonable option, as scrubbing it daily in the morning before work just wasn't feasible.

Oh, yeah, that *hides* it. But doesn't *fix* it. The problem began to get rather ridiculous, and I realized that my under the plug maintenance was important, but no longer effective. The problem lay deeper.

I brought out the *big guns*. I found a long, barbed, flexible plastic stick at the hardware store that reaches way down the pipe and then pulled it back. The barbs grabbed the gunk, fish hook style, and pulled out a long disgusting mess of yuck out of the drain. I did this several times until this stick came back up clean, digging far below the surface of the tub.

I was thorough, because I wanted this tub to drain properly.

Going way beyond to a depth I hadn't gone before with this flexible plastic *thingy* was bringing up stuff I didn't have access to before but that needed to be removed.

It worked.

The whole thing drained like a charm. Now I could leave the shower curtain open during the day. The water drained fast and left the tub shiny clean. It felt great. The whole area got a good airing, and the bathroom felt bigger.

I wasn't hiding anything anymore.

Remembering how I admired the draining qualities of my tub, I paused to think about clients who come in, confused with why something has bothered them so much. They are distressed by something upsetting, but even in the midst of it, it seems out of proportion to what is happening.

You know how when you are stressed, you have your easy *go-to* strategies?

- You have a colleague who irritates you. Well, she irritates everybody, but somehow, these annoyances affect you more than others. You get so angry. So, you come home and pick up a large bag of your favorite potato chips to inhale instead of supper.
- Your wife told an embarrassing story about you, again, at the last party you went to last evening. You felt so humiliated. You had an extra 3 or 4 (or was it 7?) drinks to drown your humiliation.

- Your son's grades continue to drop, and he leaves the house without telling you where he is going. Money goes missing from your wallet. He grunts responses when you ask him questions. No pleasant conversation at all. So, you watch the shopping channel and order something that promises it will revolutionize your life. That lady on the screen promises that this vegetable chopper will fix all your problems. You want to believe her! You order something that will make your life feel better.

- Your husband complains about how much money you spend on the shopping channel. You yell back that if he was around to help with your son's troubled behavior instead of going out with his buddies, you might not need to spend so much. Your blaming and deflection get him to back off. It works. You don't need to actually discuss the money—or your excessive shopping—because the chopper didn't actually revolutionize your life.

What do you do to make yourself feel better in short term? How do you numb or distract?

My strategies? I like bacon cheddar potato chips. Or solitaire.

Both make it feel better. For an hour.

And that's *something*. Sometimes, feeling better for an hour is super helpful. (Unfortunately, these backfire, because the amount of potato chips required to make me feel better has me feel gross after. To consume only 5 or 10 just won't do.)

Even solitaire isn't innocent. Rearranging cards for a few hours to distract myself from my pain is actually numbing. It feels different if I sit down to enjoy a single game before I go do something else.

However, sometimes, those stop-gap measures work rather like just using tweezers at the top of the drain. There is relief but only very temporary.

With the facilitation of a skilled counselor, a client can explore the issues. A person can dig deeper and find some lasting shifts that allow for lasting relief.

A therapist can help a person transform and heal those wounded parts and release the power that they have over a person. A person has the innate ability to do this but having someone join for the journey provides adds understanding and insight. This allows for fundamental shifts in ways of relating to the problem or issue:

- The co-worker is still annoying, but now your irritation is fleeting, as it is with your other colleagues. The anger just doesn't get under your skin to the extent it has previously.

- You explore and remove the troubling barriers that stopped you from having hard conversations with your wife. Now you can tell your wife you don't like it when she tells that story about you. She expresses surprise that it bothers you and reassures you she won't do it again.

- You develop an understanding of yourself and a courage to have some difficult conversations with your son. He is angry, but your persistence has you understand pressures he is under with his friends. You're still working it out with him, but you and he both understand that changes are expected. It's not easy, but there is a direction. You are moving forward.

- Your husband and you stop throwing around accusations about your spending or his time with his buddies. The two of you start having genuine conversations that build trust and connection. You start working together on schedules and budgets as you reconnect.

Therapist are like the tool from the hardware store that can reach deeper into the soul than the tweezers. Rather than *stop-gap* strategies to temporarily feel better, counseling creates lasting change by going deeper.

How effectively is the water flowing in the drain of your life? Want some help with flushing it clear by going underneath to create lasting change?

Maybe some therapy to get to actually address the issue at a meaningful level?

21 Desiring more than mediocre

Many folks are bumping along through life and managing—but just OK. They are making it and getting to the end of the day without disaster. A couple is running the household well together, getting the bills paid, and the kids raised. A person gets laid off from a job, finds employment in another city, uproots and moves, and starts the new job and plugs into it, putting one foot ahead of the other.

Many people are managing just OK.

For the women and men who begin counseling, just OK just isn't good enough.

- A couple comes to see a therapist and says, "We aren't in danger of divorce. Neither of us is going anywhere. But somehow, we aren't as close as we used to be. We want something more."

- A middle-aged man says: "I can keep going to work, coming home, playing with the kids, doing some chores, and going to bed. Then, I'll do it all over again the next day. But I'm going through the motions. I make my face smile and look interested. I really feel dead inside and have for a long time. My wife doesn't know I'm here."

- A woman at the cusp of retirement says, "I've been working towards this moment all my life. Freedom. Lots of time and a bit of money to have the freedom to do my own thing. But I'm clueless. I don't know what *my own thing* is because I've spent decades doing what my family needs me to do. It's not that I can't do it. I just don't know how to do it so it's meaningful and rich."

There is no crisis here. Nobody's falling apart. Nothing is doom and gloom. It's that people want more.

There is no single burning moment that compels these men and women to get into the therapy office. No *bring me to my knees* crisis, or heart stopping tragedy. Some come because of an ongoing simmering desire to not settle for something that feels vaguely uncomfortable, or somewhat empty.

Sometimes, it's the lack of anything that compels people to go and work things out with a therapist.

- Being in the same job for a long time may put you at the top of the salary bracket and give you an extra week's vacation. But you may wonder if you are trading in your vitality for these comforts.

- Going to the same family gatherings where they treat you in the same disrespectful way year after year is painful. You've long ago noticed that with enough glasses of wine, the edge comes off and you show up again next time. It's OK—or is it?

- You parent the kids, have a great spouse, have enough money to pay the mortgage and go on a vacation every year. It feels like you are the picture in the dictionary beside the term: *has it all*. But somehow, you're feeling dissatisfied in a way that doesn't fit the picture.

Getting along OK is adequate for many people. But maybe it's not sufficient for you.

There are years, when the snow has piled high in winter, and the warm spring comes balmy and sudden, that the folks in my city worry about basement flooding. During those times, like many of the others around, I become one of those people who rushes to the basement on first entering my house, hoping it is dry.

I feel just slightly closer to my ancestors who were farmers. I grew up hearing people talk about going to take a walk around the land or check out the crops. I worried about my house during the years I was a single mom. I was in a cute little house close to the river (read: *low ground*) that was poorly landscaped. Ideally, the ground slopes away from the house towards the streets and the drainage. In my house, the yard was contoured to be rather like a saucer around the house, collecting the water as the snow melted. The snow would pile at the edges when people cleared the sidewalks around the perimeter where the snow was piled into crusty hard snowbanks higher than the center of the yard. It added yet a higher lip to hold the water close to the house.

One spring, it was especially bad. Many basements in the neighborhood were taking on water. It was in the news every night. In the evenings, before I went to bed, I got on my rubber boots and jacket, and grabbed my flashlight for one last loop around the yard to *check out my land.* (Hey, I know it was a small yard, but technically, it was my land—or *mine and the bank's,* anyway). My sons and I were doing what we could to off-load the water. It was a family adventure. It was rather like I would read about in stories of pioneers where all members of the household banded together to desperately save the homestead from the latest travails that befell them.

We started off by scooping the water over the snow banks—trying to get rid of the large pools of water that took over our yard and threatened to overwhelm our foundation's ability to stay dry. The shovelling worked for the first few days when it first started to melt. It was manageable to shovel water together two or three times per day.

We kept a careful eye on what we came, not-so-affectionately, to know as *Lake Bergen,* our family name at the time. The yard had become a body of water. We would watch her size and depth develop as the vast amounts of snow continued to melt.

On the weekend, the rising waters made shovelling seem rather like trying to empty a bathtub with a spoon. The rate of melting was rapid. We got a lot water shovelled to the street, but our best efforts at shovelling didn't seem to put a dent in the water level. The melting rate exceeded our ability to shovel it during our two-a-day shifts before supper and before bed.

All that shovelling was modestly effective, but simply not efficient.

We could have kept shovelling, but we decided to change strategies. Something completely different. It meant we put the *scoop and dump* process with our shovels on hold.

When shovelling could not keep up, my kids and I spent a day chopping passages in the ice. We got out the axe and chipped through the smaller but still significant snow-now-turned-ice drifts. We sought to create a little path for the water to escape through the snowbank to the street away from the house into the city sewers. Ice-chipping a narrow crevice was brutal work that took several hours. There was a significant level of satisfaction in creating the path in the ice bank to the street although it didn't come immediately. We worked for a lengthy spell without a drop being drained. Chopping, clearing, scraping—over and over.

We weren't even confident this would be effective. We weren't sure how much water would actually leave.

We hammered a narrow route through the frozen dirt to create a downward path for the water to go. After a time, we could see the slightest trickle that started down the meager path we created. Then we went to bed.

It started with a dribble.

But over the hours while we slept, the magic happened. When water travels, it develops its own momentum. What started as a very narrow trickle increased overnight with the erosion that comes with water continually flowing down and eroding the ice as it travelled toward the sewer.

Two days later, what we had come to know as Lake Bergen in front of the house, had significantly reduced in size and depth, even as snow continued to melt into it. This was due to the human-made River Bergen. Over time, River Bergen made itself wider and wider, and more effective at draining the water out of Lake Bergen.

We didn't need to shovel anymore.

It was *ridiculous* how proud we were of our improved strategy.

It seems to me that life can be like that.

Clients come telling us how very hard they work at a situation. They put in lots of effort but are concerned or even terrified at the lack of significant movement on the issue.

In therapy, they talk about it, get another perspective, process the issue through a different lens and look at it with the support of a counselor in a fresh way. Potentially, it allows the way for a whole different strategy.

Often, after a first session, it's a somewhat like the axe is starting to create the path, but nothing can drain yet. That's when a skeptic can declare, "See, I knew this counseling thing was pointless—what good can talking about it do?"

But the fun starts when new understanding comes. New strategies start being used in neat ways and then the water starts flowing. Sometimes, it's because a client goes home to try an experiment or follow through on some homework that the client and therapist have talked about. Other times, a client can find themselves spontaneously making different choices because of the way the therapy session created internal shifts.

Clients come into therapy saying, "I came for help in one area, but I'm loving what is happening in another area in my life that I haven't even talked about." The path becomes wider and things happen, even without deliberate effort.

≪≫

Picture this. You are in a lawn chair beside a large man-made lake. It's pretty enough. There are children playing and laughing. It's pleasant sitting there. But there is very little beach, and it's got lots of sharp pebbles. The mosquitos are plentiful, so you are sticky from bug spray. There are algae in the water with a sign at water's edge that some may have a skin reaction after swimming. But there you sit, enjoying the landscape.

Now pan out with a larger view, rather like a camera on a drone that flies above, seeing a much broader view of the landscape. Behind where you are sitting in a lawn chair is a steep hill. It rises sharply and has some boulders that make it intimidating. That man-made lake now looks small, but it is nestled in that valley, making it pleasurable enough.

The drone rises higher, with a still yet larger panoramic view of the larger vista. On the other face of that steep, rocky hill is the ocean. Beautiful, blue-green ocean with a sandy coastline that stretches as far as the eye can see.

The water is transparent, giving a clear view to the sandy bottom and of the fish who swam magically in schools. White, padded lounging chairs are scattered along the expansive smooth sand, with beautiful thick beach towels hanging over the top of each. The scene is exquisite.

How many of us settle for sitting by a pond when the vast ocean is just over a hill? To be sure, a difficult hill is challenging to traverse. But it is possible to climb with a guide who knows the path.

Ready for a hike?

Section V Special Interest: The Counseling Conundrum

I like the key fob I have for my car that has me lock the car from the outside of the vehicle. After I am out of it. With the keys in my hand.

Scatterbrained people like me really appreciate that the very device that will let me lock the door is *in my hand* when I lock it.

Before door locks became electronic, we manually locked the door before we left the vehicle. When I locked the car door from the inside as I was getting out of the car, I needed to remember to take my keys with me.

I remember on one occasion, as I was juggling cranky children out of car seats as well as a diaper bag and grocery sacks, I swung the door shut. Before the door closed, but after I put my shoulder into shutting it, I saw my keys on the front seat of the car.

It was like one of those movies—things seemed to happen in slow motion. There was this split second when my keys were not yet locked in the car. However, I didn't have hands available that could stop the door from closing.

It was inevitable. I locked my keys in the car.

This then is the predicament:

- I require the keys to unlock the door
- I can't get to my keys because the door was locked.

A *conundrum* if there ever was one.

This is the part of therapy that no one talks much about.

Therapy often is such a riddle. The very symptom which your family is encouraging you to address in the therapy is the one that makes it hard to book and show up for the counseling session.

- The lethargy and low energy make it hard to do anything. How can therapy help if it feels as if getting out of bed is such a chore that getting to the appointment seems impossible?

- If your stomach turns and roils anytime you do something out of your small and familiar routine, how can you do something brand new and terrifying like therapy?

- When you spend your days making sure you "never" think about the worst moments in your life, why would you go to a counselor to actually talk about those experiences and their impact? Those moments may well control the way you move through your day, but you intentionally avoid every contemplating them directly— so talking to a therapist is out of the question.

- One of the symptoms of addiction is denial. How is anybody supposed to say, "I need help," when the hallmark of their life is, "I'm fine—I don't know why you are so upset!"

- If talking about challenges is impossible with your spouse on your own, how can you talk about those same challenges with your spouse and a total stranger? If you can't agree on much, how are you supposed to agree to go see a therapist?

One of my favorite quotes of all time comes from a book called *The Shack*. The author writes: "I suppose since most of our hurts come through relationship, so will our healing."[vii]

And there's the rub.

How can it be possible to let a relationship with a therapist give you the possibility of healing when it is likely that it was a relationship that created the pain in the first place?

Fair question.

We got into the car, despite the fact the keys were in the car. I called the local Automobile Association. The guy had a tool he slid up and over the closed window and used it to push on the lock to unlock it.

Let me just say I'm glad he works for the good guys, because he had the ability to get into the car in less than a minute. We found a way.

It wasn't easy, but there was a way.

Let's identify a way to get you the help you need.

22 Counseling for Depression: The hardest part is just getting there

Imagine a person interested in driving a car. She lives in a city where getting around is hard with lots of freeways and poor public transit. Her budget is limited, and a vehicle is not in the budget. She works at a business close to her home and doesn't pursue career development because other jobs in her field aren't realistic to travel to each workday. The woman is often home alone on the weekends. When friends invite her to events she declines. It's too much hassle to attend given the complexity of getting there and home without her own vehicle. She has trouble saving for a vehicle because she buys groceries from the local deli rather than the big box store miles away and so has an exorbitant grocery bill. The lack of a vehicle at her disposal shapes her life every day. She is home more than she'd like to be and feels trapped.

One day, her grandma passes away. In her will, grandma has bequeathed this woman her little car! This car is hers to drive as her own, but it five hundred miles away, in a small remote rural town.

As soon as she can get to it, she can drive wherever and whenever she wants. This is the ticket to emerge out of her isolation! The path out of too-expensive groceries! Potentials for career development! A whole new life!!

However, the dilemma is this: how to obtain the car? How does she go get a vehicle in a remote location without her own transportation? When she doesn't have a car, she can't get to the car! It could make her want to scream and cry and explode with anger—simultaneously! She collapses on the floor of her apartment in a hopeless, helpless heap.

❧ ❧

Therapy for depression is a lot like this scenario. Painfully so.

- A mother with a colicky two-month-old that screams for hours in a stretch is exhausted. She hasn't slept more than three hours at a time for weeks. This new mom sees no way out. She hasn't showered in days. It seems to her the enormous pile of laundry to be folded is exceeded by the humongous pile that has yet to be washed—and all of it overwhelming—so why even start? The family has been living on heated soup from a can and peanut butter sandwiches because she has no energy to make meals. She *knows* she is a failure as a mother and as a human being. This mom hasn't been out of the house for weeks, and won't let anybody in. She's ignoring calls from others, even those that are asking to come by to hold her crying infant to give her a break. Her husband, who seeks to be helpful in all of this, is beside himself. When he suggests she *go talk to someone* because this is hard, and maybe postpartum depression could be a part of all this—well, she goes *off* on him. She gives him the litany of things that need doing before she could possibly leave the house in a tone that is clear: Do not bring this up again. Deep down, this mother believes that nothing could help. It's all hopeless to her. Talking to someone would just make clear how pathetic she is and then they might take the baby away. This terrifies her even though there is a part of her that wonders if this baby would be better off without her as a mother.

- A young adult sits in his basement, playing hour after hour of mind-numbing video games. He loves gaming—and the interaction with others online gives him a semblance of friendships with people, or so he tells himself. He graduated from high school last year—barely. If he's honest, he hated high school because he was lonely—deeply lonely. No one knew of his isolation, even though he was going to bed later and missing too much school. He learned that when he drank, the lonely feeling went away—for an evening. Sometimes, he hung out with the guys that drank too much. And he wasn't as lonely—except the only thing they did together was hang out and drink. Now, he doesn't even see them. His mother has asked him what's wrong, but he snarls at her, and she has learned to stay away. He can tell she worries about him and makes periodic suggestions—but he has no idea what to say to her. The truth is, if he told her how hopeless it all feels, she'd probably freak out and he doesn't want to worry her any more than she already does. The world of video games is the one place he feels safe, but it also feels incredibly empty and hollow. When his mother tells him she has made an appointment to see a therapist, he knows he won't go. He isn't capable of anything. He doesn't have the words to describe what he feels and even if he did, what could anyone say to make him feel better?

- A successful engineer has now worked up to senior management of his firm. His kids are in high school, involved in many sports and artistic endeavors. His wife is happy in her career, and their mortgage is almost paid off. His head knows that everything he has ever dreamed of is now a reality. He is living his dream. But he wakes up leaden and forces himself out of bed. He watches himself take part in meetings, laughing at his colleagues' stories of the weekend as they expect him to and goes through the motions of his work to meet the deadlines. But it feels hollow. He isn't enjoying the work. His tasks take longer to complete than it used to, perhaps because he spends a lot of time staring off into space wondering if it is all worth it. He sleeps in on the weekends and only gets up when his family needs him. He snaps at his family with irritation in a way that part of him knows is unfair, but he is helpless to hold back. They just drive him to anger so often. When his wife suggests he go talk to someone because of how unhappy he is, he retorts that he has everything he has ever wanted! He's blissfully happy. Only he knows that he has just shut her down in a way she doesn't deserve. He can't look at her for the rest of the evening because he is both enraged and ashamed. But he can't be depressed—can he?

❧ ❧

Are you discouraged reading the above paragraphs? Have you begun to get a sense of how hard it is for a person with symptoms of depression to find their way to talk to someone about it? If they could talk about it, that would be a sign that the depression didn't have such a hold on their lives!

Perhaps you are glimpsing in small ways how very challenging it is for those that struggle with depression to get help.

❧❧

Andrew Solomon has a profound TED talk about his own experience of depression. In the way only a poet can describe, he said that depression is a loss of vitality. With stark candidness, he relates:

And one of the things that often gets lost in discussions of depression is that you know it's ridiculous. You know it's ridiculous while you're experiencing it. You know that most people manage to listen to their messages and eat lunch and organize themselves to take a shower and go out the front door and that it's not a big deal, and yet you are nonetheless in its grip and you are unable to figure out any way around it. And so, I began to feel myself doing less and thinking less and feeling less. It was a kind of nullity. [viii]

❧❧

Depression is often characterized as the "disease of disconnection". The tentacles of depression drag a person into the swamp of isolation. Depression is quicksand—it pulls people in and every struggle increases its hold with internal lies that say:

- "That didn't work. Nothing will work."
- "She doesn't care. He doesn't care. Why should you care?"
- "It's not worth the effort."
- "*I'm* not worth the effort."

166

- "It will never get better. It will never change. Don't even try."
- "Don't let people see how wretched I have become. They may pretend to care, but they will hurt me, just like everyone else ever has. I'm too pathetic to let anyone really see me."

When the isolation of depression doesn't allow for those lies to be reality checked, optimal conditions exist for the lies to spin tighter and tighter until they can only be perceived as unutterable truth.

Because therapy is, at its core, the creation of a helpful relationships, the very nature of depression which has people pull away from relationships makes therapy difficult to access.

The very symptoms of depression interfere with showing up for help:

- **Feelings of worthlessness:** When you feel unworthy of love, when you know no one really likes you, it's impossible to contemplate exposing yourself to one more person's judgement.

- **Loss of interest or pleasure in activities:** The lack of color in depression makes doing anything challenging. A black and white world makes a therapy appointment one more arduous task in a life of *blah*. Therapy is not *an interesting opportunity to hear another perspective*, or an *intriguing prospect to engage with someone* who may have a fresh viewpoint that could create some shifts. Therapy feels like one more hard task in a life of burden.

- **Low energy:** You may feel like you can hardly get done the things your day that have to be done. Calling to make the appointment, filling out the paperwork, and getting yourself to the office then just becomes too arduous. Therapy is an option that doesn't make it on the "to do" list,

- **Aches and pains:** The body holds the pain of depression. When your back aches, or your head pounds, or your gut twists in pain, there isn't capacity to think about talking about your problems.

- **Sleep disturbances:** How are you supposed to go to a therapy appointment when you can't get out of bed because you are sleeping the day away? It's not just a challenge—it feels unattainable. Conversely, if you've been up since 4 am every day for weeks, exhaustion has taken such hold that it's ridiculous to contemplate making an appointment after work. When your bones ache with fatigue, making a choice to go to therapy just seems absurd.

- **Difficulty making decisions:** Depression can cause you to experience diminished ability to concentrate or have you be indecisive. How is a person supposed to research to locate the right therapist at the right rate at the right time when it just all seems too much? It's just easier to not to go.

- **Helplessness and hopelessness:** If the very feature of the disease is bleakness, then therapy (along with everything else) seems useless. The very despair of depression regards therapy with great skepticism. How can anything help?

❧❦

Initiating therapy can seem nearly impossible for those in a bout of depression. But maybe the person who gave you this book is hoping you'll see this chapter and give therapy a shot. It might be that a part of you is overwhelmed with the idea of therapy—but there is a little sliver of you that recognizes it could be worth a try.

❧❦

In the woman's story—she will have a car, but only if first she can get to it—did you do what most people do? Brainstorm. Did you have some ideas when you first read the story? As someone who just wants the best for her, you don't believe she is as stuck as she feels she is. Some options might be to:

- Book a bus ticket
- Ask a friend to drive her out there
- Apply for a bank loan to rent a vehicle to drive there
- Explain the dilemma to the family and see if anyone can help
- Put a note in your grandma's town's local paper to see if anyone is heading in your direction and could drive it out, saving them the costs of the trip

And likely, you've thought of two or three additional options!

It *is* a challenge to travel to a remote location to get a car, when you don't have a car! But isn't the effort to come up with a solution, even one that requires significant effort worth it? Once she has a car, every day of her life gets easier, gives her more option, empowers her to pursue dreams.

A challenge differs from an impossibility.

Sometimes, you just need a friend or a book or a therapist to help you see it.

If you can, get support from:

- Someone in the human resource department in your factory
- A social worker or public health nurse who drops by
- A friend who cares
- A relative who sees you struggling— and is themselves impacted by your symptoms
- A colleague who recently went through a bout of depression himself
- Your family physician

These resources may be able to assist you with the internal inertia to see a counselor. They may help you find the right therapist or make the appointment with or for you. They may help you be able to hold the internal resistance—all the reasons that make therapy impossible—as valid and yet help you get there, anyway.

Doesn't it follow that if depression is a disease of disconnection, then finding and meeting with a person who specializes in connection would be the first step to climbing out of that deep, dark hole?

Hearing your fears and thoughts out loud in the presence of a non-judgemental person can be the first step in climbing the ladder out of depression. Having someone express compassion after the internal violence that depression inflicts is itself a healing balm.

Seeing a therapist can change the internal conversation. Counseling can release the confining chain of beliefs that hold your feelings hostage.

If you haven't already talked to a physician, a therapist is likely to suggest a visit to your doctor. While medication may be one topic of suggested discussion, it's not nearly the only one. It may not even be an important one. It also makes sense to consult a physician to rule out the many possible physical conditions that create feelings of depression.

When a therapist suggests a visit to the doctor, it says nothing other than: "Let's be thorough and make sure we are considering all the reasons life feels this painful for you."

Going to a therapist may seem almost unworkable, but perhaps it is just barely possible.

Seeing a therapist won't be a magic fix. Therapy isn't like a pill that has you change instantly. But seeing a therapist can, over time, reverse the descent into the vortex of darkness. As you hear yourself saying something to a therapist that together you realize has a nasty hold on you, you may find it slightly more possible to engage in your life. You listen to the critical voices differently. You are kinder to yourself in ways that improve your life. As you engage in your life, soft shades of color emerge. You may not even notice the slight color in your life until you speak of it in therapy. But, little by little, as therapy changes your life, and life changes your therapy, you get a gradual positive upward ascent of mood.

Therapy is like a ladder that the therapist will drop down into the hole of your depression. The counselor will climb down the ladder and sit with you in your darkness during your session.

At the end of the session, you may go home, but the ladder remains.

The therapist uses that ladder each week during the session to be with you. As time passes, you may let others use the ladder to be with you in between sessions. Then, over time, you may find yourself able to climb a few rungs of the ladder yourself for a while.

One day, you may find yourself poking your head out of the hole and noticing the beauty that awaits you.

Starting therapy may be one of the hardest things a depressed person may ever do. But it also may be one of the most worthwhile. Let this chapter be a vote in your life that says: "I believe you can identify a way. I hope you find a way. I think you are important and worthy of therapy. I want you to get help. I don't believe it has to stay this hard for you always. I want you to find a way to feel less miserable. If therapy is one way you may get better, then I really hope you reach out and grasp at it."

May you receive this as an invitation to reach out for the help that we all need.

23 Counseling for Anxiety: A million reasons to be anxious about therapy

Let's list some reasons for why going to a therapy session could provoke feelings of fear:

- Will I be able to locate the office?
- How will I find parking?
- Will I know what to do or where to go when I get to the office?
- How will I handle the waiting room once there?
- What will the therapist ask me, and will I be able to answer all the questions?
- What if I get so nervous in the session I have to use the restroom? What if I have a panic attack? What if I freeze and can't speak?
- What if I blurt something stupid to the therapist and embarrass myself?
- What if I don't wear the right thing and the therapist says something about it?
- What if the therapist says they can't help me because my problem is too bad?
- What if the counselor asks me to do something for homework that will be impossible?

I suspect that you can think of a few I haven't included. You are concerned therapy will create more apprehension than you can tolerate.

What if, what if, what if?

I've been a therapist long enough that therapists come as clients to see me. I had an insightful therapist ask me the first time she sat on the couch, "Do you mean to tell me that my clients go through what I just went through as I sat in the waiting room?"

She told me she had sweaty palms and butterflies in her stomach before our session began. She felt awkward while she waited and wasn't sure what to do with her hands.

It reminded me of my own anxiety that I felt when I began therapy. I have the regular run-of-the-mill angst feelings, not clinical levels of anxiety and it created significant feelings of unease to go for my first session.

That therapist's comments were impactful. They reminded me to always carefully consider pre-session anxiety. I created a book, *Is there still time to run?* [ix] for our clients to read while in the waiting room. Our clients who are anxious find it helpful to read the supportive and encouraging messages about what therapy will be like and that we honor their courage. There aren't a lot of words on each page—who can concentrate on long paragraphs when it feels like one's heart will burst out of one's chest? There are beautiful and soothing pictures as the background, because, sometimes when you worry won't make it into the session, reading becomes utterly impossible.

Our clients tell us that the book is helpful and that it understands how difficult it is to come to therapy. Oddly, when people feel understood, even just slightly, even just by a book, they feel just a wee bit better.

Just better enough—barely enough—to stay waiting in the room until the therapist comes to invite them into the session.

It's ok to find it hard to come to therapy. It's ok to go online and view therapy websites for a long time to get a "feel" for them. Sometimes, clients have told me they have read my blog for months or even years, developing a familiarity with us until they feel ready to come for a session.

The other day, I heard the counseling office line ring. Melanie, our client care manager said, "Hello, Conexus Counselling" and then it was silent.

Then she said: "Hello?" After a moment, she repeated herself, "Hello, this is Conexus Counselling." Still silence—it was evident she heard nothing.

Perhaps it was a bad cellular connection.

Perhaps it was someone wanting to inquire about counseling that suddenly found it too difficult to utter a word. Then I heard the response that Melanie gently and compassionately uttered: "We are glad you called. If it doesn't work to talk right now, please call back. We'd love to talk to you." She knew that the person just calling and saying nothing was an important step that deserved celebration.

Sometimes, people call and make an appointment, and then call to cancel it. Usually, they provide what seems to be a good reason: they got called into work, or childcare fell through. From time to time, the cancellations for those appointments are genuine but sometimes, they are a *cover story* for anxiety. They may call back to remake the appointment, but I wonder if some avoid re-booking, ashamed of their actions. They haven't a clue how much we admire people who have approached something, had to step back and then somehow dig deep to take another run at it. It's not humiliating to cancel and reschedule. It's sheer courage.

We have a policy at our counseling clinic: if you cancel with less than a business day's notice, we charge half of the session fee. The late cancel fee is for two compassionate reasons:

1. Our therapists have bills to pay and count on their clients coming. When there is a last-minute cancellation, there isn't sufficient notice to book someone else in that slot. Our therapists need compensation for their time and expertise like anyone else who earns a living.

2. Our clients often get *cold feet*. Last-minute jitters are perfectly normal. More than one client has been grateful for the policy which signals that they cannot back out of the appointment in the last moment without penalty. Knowing they will have to pay if they cancel can be the push they need to come. Generally, clients are grateful that they made it through our door.

At Conexus Counselling, we let people know that our policy is to help a client get over the anxiety that comes with a first appointment. People get anxious about the anxiety. This rapidly evolves into whirlwind of panic. The anxiety turns in on itself making an ugly spin even tighter and more fearful.

We have a variety of options open to clients who are very nervous about coming:

- A "walk'n'talk" option. After signing a waiver, we go for an hour-long walk during the session outside, weather permitting. Anxiety often creates energy internally, and this can be managed by allowing that energy to burn off with a hike through the neighborhood. Not all clinics allow for this. If you feel it would be helpful, ask about it.

- The "bring a friend" option. When it is just too hard to go to therapy alone, bring a friend. Again, different clinics may have different policies, but ask if you can bring the support you need. At our office, people can bring a friend or family member for support. Depending on what the client chooses, the friend travel with them to the office, sit with them in the waiting room, and sit vigil there during the session. Or the friend can come in with them to the session and stay during the introduction. Maybe this friend will be there for the first few minutes while the client gets used to the space and may decide to proceed on their own. Perhaps the friend is there for the full session, helping to answer questions and voicing concerns and questions on behalf of the client. At our clinic, we trust the client to recognize what is right for them and make these decisions.

- The "record the session" option. For clients who are anxious, they can find that their memory doesn't serve them well after the session. They can't remember what I've said, or what they found important. Occasionally, one of us will take notes for the client to take home. Other times, clients have asked if they could record the session on their phone. There are legitimate reasons that not all therapists allow for a recording of the session. However, if you expect this will be helpful, determine if recording your session is a possibility.

- The ***overt*** *I'm anxious* option. When anxiety becomes intolerable in session, clients tell me they are melting down/freaking out or whatever term feels right. Before we do anything else, we acknowledge the anxiety and deal with it: slow breathing, imagery, grounding work. If you aren't familiar with these, that's fine. Your therapist should know what to do if you're anxious. The counselor will help you with in-session anxiety management as the first order of business.

- The ***covert*** *I'm anxious* option. Clients aren't as explicit about their anxiety, but they take the time needed to look around the office to get their bearings. We talk about *this and that* for a while as the client has opportunity to get somewhat comfortable with the therapist. Clients will ask questions about the process so I do more of the talking while they catch their breath. Other times, we may spend more time than normal talking about the parking situation at the office, or the weather, or the local sports team. If you need to tell me about an episode you watched last evening on Netflix for 10 minutes to get used to the session, I'm all ears!

- The "create your own solution" solution. If your therapist is open to possibility, and agreeable to creative/playful solutions, check with yourself to ask what would be helpful. What would help to make the session do-able? Clients and I have brainstormed various possibilities that make therapy more feasible considering their anxiety:
    o We have play dough in small canisters for fidgeting (it's fun too!)
    o We leave the office for a few minutes to run up and down several flights of stairs to burn off nervous energy
    o I have sat on the floor to feel less intimidating, or turned my chair facing away for clients who felt that any eye contact was too much

    o People bring in music they find meaningful, or art they have created, or letters they have written to give them something concrete to talk about

The point is, select a therapist that will understand your anxiety. Ensure your therapist has experience working with anxiety. Your counselor understands that it is part of their job to help clients that have anxiety be able to take part in counseling. It will be a partnership between the therapist and your very nervous self to get the process started.

If you're anxious about the first appointment, and your anxiety feels like a runaway freight train, all the more reason to make the appointment. Use all the support you can muster to get yourself across the threshold.

The therapist will help you from there.

24 Counseling for Trauma: Dealing with the triggers that stop you

There are some people that all can agree are trauma survivors (even if these folks often choose to not self-identify themselves publicly as trauma survivors):

- Combat military veterans
- Immigrants who fled their country because of oppression, violence and political instability
- Victims of horrific motor vehicle accidents that left them recovering for months with persisting permanent injuries
- Victims or witnesses of gruesome crimes. They may have experienced harm, or they watched others die or were witness to ghastly violence
- Sexual assault survivors

Not all who experience such trauma will experience a lasting trauma response—known as PTSD (Post Traumatic Stress Disorder). In fact, many who witness and experience horrendous trauma go on to live full lives without the periodic hijacking PTSD. They don't experience the triggers or the chronic depression and anxiety that often accompany PTSD. It is not the severity of the traumatic event that predicts whether or not the survivor will have these symptoms.

Not everybody who has suffered a terrifying experience will have persistent symptoms. But some that have experienced trauma will have their lives painfully twisted around the memories.

There are also trauma survivors that have lasting trauma symptoms that don't always recognize those symptoms as arising from trauma:

- Growing up in a home with an alcoholic parent or grandparent. When the family rules of addiction are: "Don't talk, don't think, don't feel," how is a person able to understand that even though he wasn't violent, he wasn't present and available—and that matters? When her drinking had her disappear into her bedroom for days at a stretch, and a person is left to fend for oneself and the siblings—would they even know how frightening that is for a young child? Would that child let him or herself remember how difficult that was? Would that child even recognize how hard it was?

- Being pressured for sex, being called names, and consistently and subtly belittled by a former girlfriend. When men grow up in a culture where they cannot admit abuse, how is he supposed to know that this shapes a person?

- Being unpopular in grade school, with people making fun of a person's glasses, your skin color or even a strong aptitude for math. No one named it bullying back then, and everyone wrote it off as *being a baby* when that person brought it up.

Most people who struggle with symptoms of trauma would never see their trauma in news headlines. Trauma may be deeply painful without being dramatic to the outside observer. Many people experience symptoms of trauma without ever recognizing them as arising out of earlier experiences that their brains encoded as traumatic.

But—trauma is trauma.

Trauma teaches our brain powerful lessons. Our brains are wired, foremost, to keep us alive. There are parts of our brain that steer us away from danger beyond our conscious awareness. Our nervous systems not only protect us from real and present danger, but from perceived and possible danger.

- A child bitten by a dog becomes frightened and anxiously avoids all dogs. Further, dreams of dogs are, by definition, nightmares. And even discussions of dogs are off limits because they send the child into uncontrollable tears
- A person falls through ice on the river and, narrowly escaping death, is pulled out by rescue personnel narrowly escaping death. It's understandable when no amount of objective knowledge about the safe thickness of the ice will get this individual skating on the river the next year. They may avoid all winter sports. They may even avoid watching a sports channel that has winter sports.

When there is a topic that creates cold shivers within you, when there is a story that you can't bear to remember, never mind speak of, going to a therapist to talk about it seems counterintuitive. Therapists invite you to *talk about your problems,* don't they? Then it surely seems foolish to spend time with a therapist, when you order life in ways to not talk or think or remember those experiences.

Therapy is for a person's good. While counseling often isn't uncomfortable, it is **not** re-traumatizing. Therapy can be difficult, but if you find your symptoms of trauma getting worse, something needs to change. Talking about it may not seem like a good idea, but the symptoms of PTSD can include:

- Nightmares
- Cold sweats
- Flashbacks
- Anger outbursts
- Shallow relationships
- Avoidance of triggers
- Substance use/abuse
- Insomnia

- Anxiety
- Depression
- Dissociation

—those are no picnic either, are they?

Therapists who are experienced in working with those who have trauma know that to ask details of the story of the traumatic experience early in therapy is **not** helpful. Some clients will come feeling like they are *supposed* to narrate the most terrifying moments of their lives to get better. Often, if clients feel like they need to *start spilling it all* therapists will stop clients. It's important to **not** tell the horrific, traumatizing stories early in therapy—**not** because they are *too hard to hear*, but because they are *too hard to tell*.

Therapy from counselors familiar with trauma-informed therapy will focus first on resourcing the client as they deal with their symptoms. Trauma-informed therapy supports a trauma survivor as they negotiate their day-to-day existence, helping them to feel less isolated and more supported. The relating of the specific details either happens much later in therapy or not at all.

If a therapist asks you to tell the story of that which traumatizes you, inquire if they are familiar with therapy with trauma survivors. Decline to tell the story if you don't feel ready. If you perceive that the nightmares will be too intense, or it will be too hard to function in the days following, that is a flashing red sign to not talk about it. Listen to your gut and let your therapist know that you won't let the therapist override your inner sense of knowing. The conversation can focus on the part of you that knows you need to keep your foot on the brake.

Look for a therapist experienced in working with trauma if you are worried about talking about the painful stories.

So much of what creates trauma happens within the context of human relationships:

- A spouse's infidelity
- Racism, homophobia, misogyny
- Bullying
- The carnage created in relationships as the result of an addiction
- Abuse of any kind (physical, emotional, financial, spiritual) from anyone (partner, parents, boss, etc.)

People avoid experiences that feel, sound, or look like the trauma they experienced. Frankly, often it was a relationship that was harmful. So, for many trauma survivors it would likely be potentially be very triggering to talk to anybody—especially a therapist—about the trauma. There may be ways in which a potential client (consciously or beyond conscious awareness) has learned:

- Not to get too close to people
- Avoid letting others in to access tender parts of themselves
- Not believing people will be supportive
- Assuming others will be judgemental, critical, or mean
- Simply not trusting that *anybody* will act in your best interests—including a counselor

Instinctively, as a trauma survivor's brain seeks to keep them safe, that brain often says: *"Therapy is not safe"*. Our brains would far rather be wrong by keeping us away from something that could be safe than be wrong by allowing us to do something that seems safe, but turns out to be harmful. **Brains err on the side of caution** and so generally, brains are suspicious of therapy. Brains all over the globe tell the heads they inhabit: *"Do not go to therapy. Do not trust this person. Do not trust the process. Stay safe by pulling back from anything vulnerable like therapy."*

Let me give you some information about trauma-informed therapy that may help you talk to the part of your brain that says: "NO WAY" to therapy.

There are 5 principles of trauma-informed therapy that competent therapists that can work effectively with you will know:

1. **Safety:** Therapists will instinctively know that therapy is risky and has an inherent danger for you. They will create safety for you. They will do that in a whole variety of ways. The counselor will let you know about their style so you know what to expect. They will invite you to ask questions whenever you have one. They will ask you to tell them when something is uncomfortable or you don't want to answer a question. At our practice, we have a lot of information on the website to allow people to know what to expect. We have a book in our waiting room[x] that educates people about what to expect in the session that you might find helpful. A trauma therapist will notice when you start to get upset or disconnect from reality and work to help you start to feel OK again by grounding you. They will understand that in order to proceed forward, they can't push you. A therapist will know that a sense of safety builds slowly. Trust is built over time. Trustworthiness is important. Therapists know it requires some time in therapy before the hard stuff can be approached, and we are prepared to wait.

2. **Choice:** Trauma therapists understand that often trauma was as difficult as it was because you were trapped. You had no options and you felt cornered. Trauma-sensitive therapy will provide you with the ability to make decisions in therapy. Some of our clients like to walk outside during their sessions. Other clients request that we not look at them, or avoid using certain words, or they like to talk about something innocuous for a few minutes at the beginning of each session. Some like lots of humour, some none at all. Some prefer to pay at the beginning of a session, or book at the end of the hour—or the email us the following day. Whenever it works for us and is helpful for the client, we work to accommodate the needs of the client.

3. **Collaboration:** Trauma therapy happens with close cooperation between therapist and client. The therapist checks in with the client to see how they are doing or asks for signals if something gets too uncomfortable. We establish goals and strategies that work together with you, monitoring regularly and inviting feedback to ensure that a client isn't flooded. Trauma therapy isn't done *to* a person, but rather *with* a person. The therapist is attuned to the client and makes constant adjustments as each conversation unfolds.

4. **Trustworthiness:** A therapist will know that a sense of safety builds as trust is built, over time. Trustworthiness is important. At our practice, we seek to be upfront, clear and consistent to avoid surprises around policies regarding cancellations, scheduling, payment etc. We show up for appointments as scheduled. I ask clients to tell me if they feel like I said something hurtful or offensive so that we can talk about it. I will apologize if we discover I made a mistake. While therapists do their best, they are also human, and so will make mistakes. Give your therapist an opportunity to own their error. We know that trust is developed like drops into a bucket, and that breaking of trust empties it by the cupful. We invite any perceived or actual breaking of trust to be brought up in the therapy to clarify misunderstandings and to repair any ruptures in the relationship between therapist and client.

5. **Empowerment:** Therapists who have worked with survivors of trauma know that there is a wisdom and extreme capability that has helped a person survive. The strength and insight of a trauma survivor is respected and valued. A therapist partners with the resilient and courageous parts of the client to do therapy. It only makes sense to include the client in the decisions, and to value all of who the client is. We build on the survivor's natural and real strengths as therapy moves forward.

Therapists don't relate to you out of these principles as a *gimmick*. It's a fundamental style of clearly relating to you in a way that understands: *Safety first.* We relate to you out of these five principles because it's how we show that we care.

It's not only acceptable, it's expected for survivors of all sorts of trauma to be skeptical of therapy. Suspicion and hesitation for therapy is standard for trauma survivors. Make sure you do your research. Identify the qualifications and experience of the therapist. Do what's necessary to soothe the part of your brain that has concerns. Address those concerns respectfully with knowledge. Assure your brain that you are keeping yourself safe by choosing a therapist carefully and that you will advocate for yourself in therapy to maintain safety. The therapist that is suitable for you will not only tolerate caution but encourage you to be careful.

Go ahead and take care of your brain and the rest of you. Listen to your body and take care of it. Help it learn to deal with the trauma in a way that is, in itself, is a lesson in calming that terrified part that only wants the best for you.

25 Counseling for Addictions: Getting help for a problem you can't admit you have

If you're reading this chapter, chances are that you are angry. Enraged. Furious. Someone has suggested that you get treatment for an addiction. You might think:

- "How dare they hint I have a problem with _______?"
- "Don't they know how hopeless it is for me to stop? If I could stop, I would have stopped a long time ago!"
- "What do they know about how much/little I use?"
- "They are so ignorant of my back story. If they knew what I had to deal with, then they would get it and stop griping at me."

Or you're incensed at yourself that you have allowed yourself to get to where you fear this chapter may be for you.

Can you feel your rage, let it be exist and also to read this chapter? Can you honor both your feelings and the feelings of the person who expressed the concern?

No one signs up to have a problem with alcohol or gambling or meth or shopping or pornography or food or sex or prescription pain medication or anything else.

No one, including you *wants* to be an addict.

Everyone wants to believe that they are in control and that they could stop if they wanted to stop. (They just don't see the need to stop, so they won't.)

Everyone wants to believe that no one understands.

When someone asks *how much* _______ (alcohol, weed, shopping, etc.), they tell them, *mostly*. (Except not *exactly* the whole truth, because if they did, others would make such a big deal of it, wouldn't they?)

❧❧

One of the most poignant learning moments about addiction happened in the couples counseling class I took for my therapy degree.

The professor described how one of his mentors, a therapist, had a plastic blow-up beer bottle in his office. Inflated, this bottle of brew was about 6 feet tall, and more than a foot across. It took a fair chunk of space in the corner of the therapy office. The therapist would refer to it when he had a couple come for therapy presenting with problematic alcohol use in the relationship.

The reality of addictions is this: Almost always, when someone expresses a concern regarding an addiction, the person who is accused of the problem minimizes and belittles the issue. Often, the person who experiences the most pain of addiction most overtly is not the addict him/herself. Rather, the one who is most vocal about the pain of addiction is the partner/parent/child of the addicted person. The person addicted to a substance or behavior also experiences pain creating the need for the addiction and resulting from the addiction, but one feature of the addiction itself is denying this pain.

My professor described how the therapist worked with this couple—the wife was convinced that her husband's use of alcohol was devastating in their marriage. The therapist asked her to position the bottle where she best felt it represented its presence in their relationship. The wife leaped up to claim that monstrous bottle and plunked it in the middle of the loveseat between them. She sat back down, squished into the corner of the two-seater couch—because there was now very limited space for her.

The therapist asked if there was anything else to sculpt this scene to further depict the relationships between the couple and the bottle. She again nodded. Without hesitation, she took her husband's hands and pulled them so that his arms were wrapped around the bottle.

As he embraced the bottle and she perched uncomfortably on the far end of the sofa, she said with pained and weary satisfaction: "Yes, this is what my marriage feels like."

Very simply, addiction is when a person:

- Finds temporary relief from pain or discomfort or experience pleasure from a substance/process/activity
- Experiences cravings for the activity/substance
- Subjects themselves to long term negative impact by continuing this behavior
- Has an inability or lack of desire to stop despite the negative consequences[xi]

Addictions are an attempt to deal with pain by not dealing with the pain. They create a bigger problem even as they are an attempt to solve the pain problem.[xii]

The paradox of addiction treatment is this: To deal with the addiction, one has to deal with the very pain that one has been avoiding by having the addiction in the first place. The pain felt overwhelming or there weren't adequate resources to deal with it prior to the addiction and the addict still does not have the internal resources.

The route out of addiction is to learn to deal with the pain. That is daunting. Exponentially disheartening and discouraging. Additionally, an addiction is hard to stop. The body is used to the substance and needs it. Withdrawal can be agonizing.

Sobriety seems too much. To quit is too hard. Often, previous efforts to stop using the substance or activity has been a miserable failure. It just seems the attempt to stop again is to set oneself up for failure and create yet more pain. Failure hurts. So much of addiction arises out of people despising themselves and being disappointed in themselves. Repeated failure to stop the addiction further feeds into this self-hatred.

Addictions can reach a threshold where it becomes intolerable. The impact on a person's life is devastating:

- Getting fired from employment
- The credit cards reach their limit, and the line of credit is maxed out
- Losing your license for a serious driving violation
- Your spouse leaves you
- A medical crisis with a narrow escape from death

Sometimes, people call this *hitting bottom*—when it seems the only option is to pursue treatment.

Often, though, there isn't an enormous tragedy that precipitates the crisis. Rather, it's a slow dawning, or a point where a person just says, "Enough". It may seem no different from a thousand other moments, but this time, it feels distinctive:

- A person is sick and tired of *being sick and tired*
- The weight gain has continued, and you aren't willing to go up yet another pant size
- You have had enough of the four walls of your basement and you desire more out of life than just clicking the buttons on a video game controller
- The substances mellow you out and have pulled you out of life in a way that you're no longer willing to tolerate: no more missed promotions, no further lost opportunities for a relationship with a partner, or no more missing the pursuit of goals that align with your values.

One hallmark of addiction is that there is *negative long-term impact*. Your overuse/misuse of a substance, compulsive spending or use of pornography, etc.:

- is threatening the end of a relationship
- has your children distance themselves
- strains your finances
- preoccupies you to the extent that you don't attend to the necessities of life
- impacts your health
- has you feel worse about yourself (which is numbed for a short while when you engage in the addictive behavior only to reappear with a vengeance after)

Talk to any person who has fought the hard-won battle to reach sobriety and maintain it. They will tell you it was hard but worth it.

This book generally is about helping the reader make an informed and wise choice regarding therapy with a counselor at a clinic. This chapter on addictions encourages you to choose the appropriate treatment, which may not always be having *one* counselor with whom to talk. For an addiction, the right level of intervention may be a treatment center, a hospital program, inpatient detox, or a remote residential setting. A counseling session once per week may be woefully inadequate.

Seeing a therapist weekly to get a handle on late night shopping that has gotten out of hand may work. Talking to a counselor about how much fast food you've taken to eating may be the right venue. *If* the addiction's hold is not longstanding and the person is able to recognize the hold of the behaviors early, less intensive intervention *may* be sufficient. Booking sessions with a therapist at a clinic may address those behaviors and the underlying pain that those behaviors intend to relieve.

However, there are other situations, when you are struggling with addictions where counseling will only throw a bucket of water at a raging fire.

While not useless, counseling may be inadequate to treat a long-standing entrenched addiction. Much more intensive treatment may be required.

Yes, this means that more friends and family will be aware of your situation. To attend a treatment program of some sort:

- means a heavy financial investment, perhaps a leave of absence from your job, or losing your job altogether
- implies it will become more public that you have an addiction
- will also make more public that you have the courage and desire to do what it takes to get the help you require.

Reaching out for help is admirable. It invites support. It is an indication of character strength.

If upending your life gets you on the road to getting your life back, isn't that worth it?

Some forms of addictions:

- have danger during the withdrawal period
- are tenacious in their grip
- have been in place for so long it requires that significant support during withdrawal and early recovery
- require radical withdrawal from the community and the supply of the substance
- necessitate a significant amount of support that a counseling office is not in a position to provide

If someone gave you this book because they recognize that addictions come between you, **pay attention**. If they say your use breaks their heart or makes their life miserable, **listen up**. Their experience isn't right or wrong: it's *true* for them. Their experience of how you related to a drug, alcohol, work, shopping, video games, pornography, food, sex, or ________ is valid for them. By dismissing their experience of your addiction, you dismiss them.

Relationships cannot survive dismissals indefinitely.

As you care about the one who loves you, allow their perspective to impact you. Trust that the very circumstances of addiction mean that it can be difficult for you to identify how you and the people that surround you are impacted.

Nobody approaches a person to accuse them of addiction without serious misgivings. The brave and loving person who approached you did so because they care enough to risk a hostile reaction, to meet your resistance. They expected it was likely that you would ridicule or shame them.

The person giving you this book with lines highlighted in this chapter didn't expect the reaction would go well and *they did it anyway.*

Because **they care** about **you**.

Can you let that land on your soul?

Johann Hari, a journalist, has spoken with many of the top addiction experts in the world. He has given a TED talk and written about addictions. I think his most quoted line is this:

"The opposite of addiction isn't sobriety. The opposite of addiction is connection."[xiii]

Sobriety is important, to be sure. But it is not possible to underestimate the significance of connection. We all need:

- a place where to belong
- a space where we can make known some of the ugliest parts of ourselves and rather than receive judgement, feel a response of compassion
- someone with whom we can bounce ideas—where the spinning thoughts have a place to unwind
- a safe place to share pain, to learn how to hold our own pain, to have someone to trust with hearing the pain.

A therapist, either in a treatment center, detox center, or clinic can be the entry point to finding that journey toward meaningful connection. When you are meaningfully connected, you will find ways of holding your pain as the compassionate presence that occurs in connection allows you to learn.

Expect that the therapist will encourage you to broaden the circle of connection—a single therapist is not sufficient to support a person on the path out of serious addiction. Besides writing in a journal or reading or other solitary activities, therapists are likely to encourage group therapy, Alcoholics Anonymous or other support groups, a treatment center, and/or family therapy. It's important to bring others into your healing journey. You will feel uncomfortable, you will resist it, but connecting with family, friends and others who struggle is essential.

Treatment won't be easy, but you will get your life back.

26 Counseling with Couples: If you aren't both happy, it isn't a happy relationship

Couple/family therapy is a unique conundrum because it involves more than one person in the client unit. Both have to agree to create the consensus for couple therapy to begin.

This is the problem: The very reason for therapy is that the two of you have some trouble understanding and collaborating with each other.

The two of you are having trouble understanding each other and working together—and now have to get on the same page to go see a therapist together.

It often strikes me we live in a culture that believes in prevention. We:

- get oil changes for our cars
- go to the doctor and dentist for checkups to address problems in our bodies and teeth
- get insurance in case our house burns down
- set timers on our phones so as not to forget things
- have an alarm on our smoke alarm to warn us when the battery needs replacing.

There are so many checks and balances to help us stay on top of things to ensure our safety. We believe in problem prevention. We address issues when they are small so as not to allow them to get away on us and create much greater quandaries down the road. So why do so many couples allow their relationship to deteriorate for years without tending to it? We consider an intimate partner relationship to be the most important relationship in a person's life. Why does anyone let it fall apart under their noses? Why does anyone push away the wounding and let it fall apart behind their backs?

We also recognize the need for experts:

I go to a:

- Hairstylist to cut my hair
- Mechanic to fix my car
- Lawyer to draw up a will
- Real estate agent to sell my house
- Doctor to tell me what the pain means and what the recommended treatment is
- Teacher to instruct my children on trigonometry and calculus

Why wouldn't I also go to a relationship expert to help me when my relationship is showing signs of deterioration?

My husband, Jim and I, made an agreement with each other when we got married: *If either of us says we need to go see a marriage therapist, the other one is obliged to cooperate with the process.* **No exceptions.**

Frankly, it is more likely that Jim will pull the trigger on seeing a therapist.

Here's the deal: I work with words and conversations and relationship dynamics for a living. I know my way around a marital conflict like nobody's business. It's my job. We have discussed the possibility that without my realizing it, I could talk him out of his feelings. Or I might work my way out of a situation in a manner that slights him and do it without either of us even noticing it. This disadvantage he has because I am a therapist means that our relationship could become unfair for him and I might not even be aware. He might not even understand what is happening. He'd just know that it wasn't good. For that to happen falls outside of my values. I don't want to hurt him deliberately or inadvertently. Intentional and unintentional pain hurts the same.

I want Jim to love our relationship. I hope that if I am doing something destructive without being aware of it, that he will call me on it, on his own, or with the help of a therapist. So, when I heard friends had this understanding, I thought it would be great for us to adopt it, too.

If either of us feels:

- in over our head,
- repeatedly that we aren't heard,
- something critical in our relationship is missing and our efforts to figure it out are unsuccessful,
- something isn't working and nothing is working to get it working again,

then we will go to a therapist together.

Even if we:

- don't want to go
- are embarrassed
- think it's silly

We will go to couple therapy, regardless of our discomfort or distaste, because we have decided in advance our relationship will be more important than our desire not to go to a therapist.

It will be difficult for me to go see a therapist in our city. I know a lot of the more experienced ones personally and so to identify a suitable counselor for us will be a challenge. Our agreement makes sure that I won't use this challenge as an *empty excuse* not to go to counseling should he feel it would be valuable.

Going to a couples therapist is often something one partner doesn't want to do. However, the request from the partner doesn't arise in a vacuum.

196

The request signals a distance that exists that can't be overcome, or that a rupture has occurred that hasn't been repaired.

Saying **no** therapy isn't just saying, *"Don't make an appointment."* When a partner disregards the request for therapy, the implication, however unintended is this: *"My discomfort/dislike for therapy is more important than your concern or hurt regarding our relationship."*

That is a painful message to receive.

It's a dangerous message to send.

It's a catastrophic way to live.

Therapy is uncomfortable. We are getting to the end of a book whose content explores why this discomfort is worthwhile. Most don't anticipate a therapy appointment like an evening out or a special date. When you reject this uncomfortable act of therapy, the implicit message is that you don't value the relationship more than you dread the discomfort.

A therapy session with me has unfavorably been compared to a root canal. People mention this to me with a chuckle, but they aren't joking, really.

I had a root canal once. It was most unpleasant. Several needles in my mouth with freezing, digging around in my gums in ways that were uncomfortable and felt unnatural. I hated the sound of that drill in my mouth—second only to the feeling of the vibration of said drill throughout my skull.

Yet, as much as I didn't like that root canal, I was grateful once it finished. The pain that had me awake at midnight, rocking in my bed in agony, disappeared. I could eat and sleep normally again.

The root canal wasn't comfortable, but it was effective in solving an important problem. It allowed me to actually live my life again.

If I need another root canal, I won't be happy. But *I will readily go.*

And if your partner asks you for couple therapy, can you say, *"Yes"* in the same spirit as I said, *"Yes"* to a root canal?

It might surprise you that counseling likely won't be about blaming you, or scolding. If you don't like the way therapy unfolds, you need to let your therapist know. Collaboration between the three of you will be key to couple therapy success. You will shape the therapy sessions along with your spouse.

❧❧

We all know someone that had a little lump that they ignored. It **probably** was nothing, and they didn't want to make a fuss about *nothing*— neither did they go to the doctor because they **dreaded** the idea that it might be something. They hoped if they would ignore it, it would go away.

For some that works. For others, that lump turns into an advanced cancer that not only no longer can be ignored, it can no longer be effectively treated. A cure is no longer possible because of the advanced stage of the cancer's growth.

I've worked with too many marriages who ignored what they hoped was *nothing* and by the time they come to see me, there is no meaningful relationship left to work with. They've waited years too long, the ruts of painful patterns are too deep and the wounds they've inflicted actively or passively are excruciating. Trust can never be rebuilt.

If your spouse has asked you to go to therapy, listen. Recognize the danger in hoping that if you wait long enough, it will *blow over*.

❧❧

A couple of points to think about with couple therapy:

- Avoid beginning therapy as a means to determine "who is right, and who is wrong". A therapist is not a judge. The task of a therapist is to improve your relationship, not assign blame.
- Be prepared to listen to words that may not be easy to hear. Know that the conversation is better when responses are shaped by curiosity rather than judgement

- Usually, people have all the "communication skills" they need to go about their lives—including their marriage. The two of you had sufficient communication to date and plan your lives together. Communication skills don't decrease with marital tension, but a person's ability to access those skills does. Thinking a few "communication tools" will solve everything is often magical thinking.

- Bad choices on one spouse's part doesn't justify abuse. Ever. It is important to process what makes you mad, but a therapist will never affirm behavior such as name calling, physical violence, berating and belittling. Be upfront—both of you—about abuse that exists in the relationship. Allow the therapist to work with full knowledge of the situation.

If you are reading this chapter because your spouse gave it to you and is asking you to consider couple therapy, do me a favor.

Thank your spouse. *Seriously*, yes—express gratitude.

Let your partner know that you are aware it was very brave and very kind for your spouse to give you this book. Let your spouse know that this chapter was a lot to digest and you won't be able to discuss it further just yet because you need some time to think it through.

You may have been shocked when your spouse invited you to therapy. You may have turned it down a dozen times or more in the past. You may not have understood how much struggle exists within your partner. Although it may be very challenging for you, let your spouse know that you want to understand.

Let your partner know you have pondered this, and it *matters* to you, *even if it is only because it matters to your spouse*. **I suspect you want this marriage to work as much as your spouse does.**

Knowing that your partner is asking you to read this chapter because she/he wants you to go with them to therapy may even make you furious. Your first instinct might be to hide, get drunk or pull away. Maybe you are pulled to get involved in a super big project in the garage or at work or at the community center to avoid the conversations this chapter invites. You may be pissed off because of the implications of this chapter.

Maybe you may have devoted your life to providing him/her a wonderful life with secure finances and a beautiful house. You may go together on a big vacation once a year. You may cook grand meals or make a comfortable home. There are lots of signs you can point to, to show you have tried to give your partner what you thought was a great life. When you read this chapter, it might hurt because all your good intentions won't feel good enough.

If your spouse asks you to work on your marriage now before he/she is completely burnt out, please show up? Stick with the process and you give yourself a fighting chance. You give your therapist something to work with when you come before your relationship deteriorates further. It isn't easy to agree to start counseling. If it wasn't your idea, you may have a lengthy list of concerns. Read some other chapters in this book to have some of your concerns addressed.

But consider this: To say "*yes*" to counseling is a vote for your marriage. It tells your partner you take his/her concerns seriously—and when you take your partner's concerns seriously, then your partner feels understood.

The very act of agreeing to therapy will give your spouse have an experience of being loved by you. How can your spouse feeling loved not be incredibly advantageous for the both of you?

Epilogue

What do you have to lose?

What would be the worst part about showing up at a clinic and giving therapy a shot? What could go wrong? You have the ability to express to the therapist:

- I will not answer that question
- The way you're staring at me makes me uncomfortable
- I have a bunch of questions you need to answer before I will decide if I will stay
- How do you understand that counseling can help me?
- I didn't make this appointment because I wanted to come. I'm here because my wife/father/boss said I should come. I'm reluctant. You should know that.
- I will come for one session and see how it goes.
- I've made appointments with 3 therapists, and I will choose the one I feel fits me the best
- I didn't want to come today because I'm concerned that there might be adverse effects. You need to help me make sure I don't freak out after.

There is a whole range of ways you can give your therapist a "heads up" that you are not yet jumping in with both feet.

You can start therapy with significant reservations and be vocal about them. Therapists want you to name your skepticism up front and want to talk about it.

However, the danger in saying: "I went, and it didn't work. I'm not going back," is that you didn't give it a fair attempt. Nobody would like a highly recommended restaurant if they order brussels sprouts and they've hated them all their life. And nobody can speak well of a restaurant if they've received their favorite delicious meal in front of them but never picked up a fork to taste it.

If you try therapy, be honest with yourself. Getting your body into the therapy office is not enough. You will have to actually invest. Engage with the counselor authentically and if that means challenging them because of your uncertainty, then that is the place to begin.

You don't need to start with the darkest and most intimate details. In fact, I would discourage starting with the most difficult pain in your life. *Float some trial balloons* of issues that are real but smaller in significance to see how it goes. Give yourself the gift of authentically determining if therapy could help. Go in full of with your questions, concerns, suspicions and disbelief to engage in a genuine dialogue that is open and curious. *But do go in.*

If you put nothing in, I highly suspect you will get nothing out.

If you are wondering about the value of therapy, or someone that cares deeply about you is entreating you to go, I want to encourage you to pursue it. I picture you reading this as I write this and I am encouraged by your willingness to get even this far. I wrote this book for you and desire better for you.

I believe that *you* matter. My hope for you is to live a better story—to have the adventure that you know as your life to be fulfilling, enriching, and life-giving. I want you to engage in your life and respond to the challenges that life has thrown your way in a style that has you honor your values and live your best life.

"It doesn't have to stay this way." I often utter this at the end of a first session. I mean it. I don't know what it will look like, how the client and I will change their circumstances, or even if we can change the circumstances. We *can* change the way a person reacts to the situations in their lives. We can develop strategies of resilience. We can explore parts of a person they weren't aware of that controlled their lives unknown to them. I don't know how fast it will go. I don't know how hard it will be. I don't know how it

will change. But my experience has me recognize that a client's experience *doesn't have to stay stuck*.

And I recognize that **you are worth it**. Please recognize that you can have a better life.

Go for it. Grab that better life.

About the Author

Carolyn Klassen has completed a Master of Arts degree in Marriage, Family, and Child Counselling in Fresno, California. She also has a degree in Occupational Therapy from the University of Manitoba.

She is a therapist and director at Conexus Counselling in Winnipeg.

A Certified Daring Way Facilitator, she believes that fundamentally, all of us are wired for connection, and that meaningful relationships have tremendous healing power. Carolyn taught therapeutic communication to therapy students for many years at the University of Manitoba. Carolyn now speaks widely and writes about all things **connection**.

She has a 2018 TEDx Winnipeg talk, *Learning from the sequoias: the value of interconnectedness*. She is passionate about helping people improve their relationships with themselves and each other. She has written *Nice to a Fault: Redefining Kindness in Marriage,* and *Is there still time to run?* and a weekly conversation with Hal Anderson on 680CJOB. She loves lattés, family suppers, busy bird feeders, sun porches, and watching her sons play sports.

Carolyn would be extremely grateful for you review with a comment on Amazon. You are invited to contact her at info@conexuscounselling.ca

Notes:

i Graaf, John De, et al. Affluenza: The All-Consuming Epidemic. Berrett-Koehler Publishers, 2005.

ii "Sea Turtle With One Flipper Gets Rudder Prosthetic | Nature on PBS." *YouTube*. March 24, 2014. https://www.youtube.com/watch?v=TpzATXGBIqQ.

iii "Wizard Revealed - Wizard of Oz 75th Anniversary - Own it October 1." Video file. July 17, 2013. https://youtu.be/-RQxD4Ff7dY.

iv "Learning from the Sequoias: the Value of Interconnectedness | Carolyn Klassen | TEDxWpg." Video file. October 2, 2018. https://youtu.be/S9BJjkijb2I.

v Pinker, Susan. *The Village Effect: How face-to-face contact can make us happier and healthier.* Toronto: Random House of Canada Ltd., 2015.

vi *Veggie Tales: The Hairbrush Song – Silly Song.* YouTube video, posted by VeggieTales Official, November 13, 2008, https://youtu.be/LtHr7gluh08.

vii Young, William P., Wayne Jacobsen, and Brad Cummings. 2007. *The shack: where tragedy confronts eternity.* Newbury Park, CA: Windblown Media.

viii Solomon, Andrew. "Transcript of "Depression, the Secret We Share"." *TED: Ideas Worth Spreading.* October, 2013. https://www.ted.com/talks/ andrew_solomon_depression_the_secret_we_share/transcript.

ix Klassen, Carolyn. *Is there still time to run?: A message from your therapist before your first session,* 1st ed. Winnipeg: Carolyn Klassen, 2019.

x Klassen, Carolyn. *Is there still time to run?: A message from your therapist before your first session,* 1st ed. Winnipeg: Carolyn Klassen, 2019.

xi The definitions of addiction vary only slightly, and I'm using one here that Dr. Gabor Maté uses. You can see it clearly defined here: *Russell Brand and Dr. Gabor Maté/ Damaged Leaders Rule the World.* Retrieved from: https://www.youtube.com/watch?v=C-mJnYmdVmQ on September 18, 2019

---

^{xii} To further understand this, you may wish to view: *What is Addiction? [Gabor Maté]*. Retrieved from: https://www.youtube.com/watch?v=T5sOh4gKPIg on September 16, 2019

^{xiii} Johann Hari, "Transcript of "Everything You Think You Know About Addiction is Wrong"," *TED: Ideas Worth Spreading*, June, 2015. https://www.ted.com/talks/johann_hari_everything_you_think_you_ know_about_addiction_is_wrong/transcript.

www.ingramcontent.com/pod-product-compliance
Lightning Source LLC
Chambersburg PA
CBHW051511030726
47592CB00006B/2218